D1592471

50 Plus One Great Books You Should Have Read (and probably didn't)

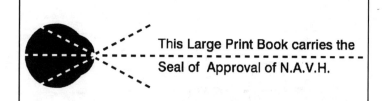

This Large Print Book carries the
Seal of Approval of N.A.V.H.

50 PLUS ONE GREAT BOOKS YOU SHOULD HAVE READ (AND PROBABLY DIDN'T)

GEORGE WALSH

THORNDIKE PRESS

A part of Gale, Cengage Learning

GALE
CENGAGE Learning

Detroit • New York • San Francisco • New Haven, Conn • Waterville, Maine • London

GALE
CENGAGE Learning

LIBRARY OF CONGRESS CATALOGING-IN-PUBLICATION DATA

Walsh, George, 1950–
   50 plus one great books you should have read (and probably didn't) / by George Walsh.
     p. cm. — (Thorndike Press large print health, home, & learning)
   ISBN-13: 978-1-4104-1254-6 (alk. paper)
   ISBN-10: 1-4104-1254-7 (alk. paper)
   1. Best books—United States. 2. Large type books. I. Title. II. Title: Fifty plus one great books you should have read (and probably didn't).
Z1035.9.W35 2009
011'.73—dc22
                   2008041280

Published in 2009 by arrangement with Encouragement Press, LLC.

Printed in the United States of America
1 2 3 4 5 6 7 12 11 10 09 08

Special thanks . . . and cheers
to the following:
Joe David and Ann Kepler

TABLE OF CONTENTS

INTRODUCTION

Simple words have had the most profound effect on the world — its history, literature, art, science, religion and economics. To know and to have read the great masters is to understand and appreciate the complex interaction of world events as they unfold. *50 plus one Great Books You Should Have Read (and probably didn't)* is the first attempt to organize the great literature, both fiction and non-fiction, in such a way as to demonstrate their world-wide impact.

Every attempt has been made to introduce readers to books and literature that is international in scope and spans the centuries. The works chosen are not necessarily the most famous — nor are their authors. Rather, they represent seminal works, masterpieces that every educated individual should have at least some familiarity with.

In a few short pages, you will learn about the authors, their background and influences, as well as a good deal about the works themselves. In many ways we have provided a very sophisticated book with many important topics — but it is presented to you in an easy-to-read reference style. While not being simplistic by any means, every effort has been make to ensure basic understanding of the authors and their works.

Please remember that we are trying to channel some of the greatest minds and the greatest works into a few pages — which is a trick in itself! Nevertheless, readers will get a treat of their intellectual lifetimes when they begin sampling the many and the variety of writers and books.

For your own enjoyment, to impress others or to improve your trivia skills, this is a wonderfully enjoyable book filled with information and insight.

Savor it; enjoy it and cherish the authors as we do. Happy reading.

George Walsh

PLUS ONE
THE BIBLE:
Old and New Testaments

THE WORKS

The Bible

The complete *Bible,* both the "Old Testament" (which comprises of 66 books) and the "New Testament" (which comprises of 27), is the effort of many different authors who wrote over a period of time estimated to be about 1,600 years.

The first five books of the "Old Testament" (Genesis, Exodus, Leviticus, Numbers, and Deuteronomy) are, by tradition, believed to have been written by the Jewish prophet and leader Moses. Moses began his writings sometime prior to 1445 B.C. and finished them approximately 40 years later with the completion of Deuteronomy around 1405 B.C. The last book of the "Old Testament" was written by the prophet Malachi; it was completed some time around 450 B.C.

The books of the "New Testament" were

bookommend.blogspot.com
↻ good ok mixed yawn ☯

written by the followers and apostles of Jesus Christ. The first four books of the "New Testament" (the gospels of Matthew, Mark, Luke, and John) are perhaps the best known, because they chronicle the life, teachings, death and resurrection of Jesus Christ. The apostle Paul is credited as the author of thirteen of the books in the "New Testament." The book of Galatians was written in 49 A.D. and is one of, if not the, earliest books in the "New Testament."

Religious dogma credits the inspiration of the Biblical authors to the divine influence of the Holy Spirit, not to conventional human wisdom. Historic events and interpretation as a result of the personal experiences of the Biblical authors were probably just two of the many factors that shaped the writings that collectively became known as *The Bible.*

The Bible has variously been called Holy Writ or Divine Scripture or The Good Book — among many hundreds of descriptions. These exalted descriptions convey its importance to the world in general.

Since its creation in the centuries before and after the birth of Christ, it has been endlessly organized and reorganized. It is generally described as being in three parts: "The Old Testament," "The New Testament," and "The Apocrypha." "The Apocrypha" is not always included in modern versions, but it was translated and included in the famous King James translation of *The Bible* (1611), which is still the standard in the English-speaking world 4 centuries after it was created.

The three parts are organized by "books" (often, though not always, thought to be the work of one person); these books are subdivided into "chapters," and the chapters are divided into "verses" — not, as the name implies, poetry, but rather numerically designated sequences of a single sentence or two. This organization — thus, Matthew 4:16 — was devised to make finding individual passages of *The Bible* simple and easy for readers.

Originally written in Hebrew and Greek, *The Bible* has been translated into more than 2,000 different languages — more than any other book in history. As well, *The Bible* is the world's runaway best-seller. Since the early 19th century, when accurate publishing records started being kept, it is believed to have sold more than five billion copies.

Why this extraordinary popularity? One reason is obvious. *The Bible* is the basis of the Christian religion, and in the Western world in which we live, though that world

15

has large minorities of other religious faiths (notably Jews and Muslims), Christianity is the dominant religious faith. And Christians, to varying degrees, regard *The Bible* as the Word of God, transmitted through human beings who were divinely inspired. It includes the moral instructions and directives to which Christians adhere in their spiritual lives.

Some people would argue that, within the Western world, as well as those portions of the world in which Christianity is a minority faith, the Christian religion is dying. In Protestant countries — for example, England — most people no longer attend church or profess any Christian affiliation. In Catholic countries — for example, France — the same indifference to organized Christianity is growing. Even in the United States — the most religious country in the Western world — a good percentage of the population is secular, though not necessarily immoral or unethical: it is simply that their standards are based on philosophies other than those of traditional Christianity.

Such statistics are misleading. A belief in Evangelical Christianity and its practices is growing — in all parts of the Western world. Thus *Bible* study — and, particularly, interpretation of that study — is also increasing.

Even if one remains secular in his or her beliefs, there are still compelling reasons for modern man to be familiar with *The Bible.* The great conflicts of the new 21st century so far have been based on religion — conflicts between adherents of Christianity, Judaism, and Islam; and although it is most associated with Christianity, *The Bible* affects, is involved in, all three of these great world religions. The "Old Testament" recounts the story of the peoples of the ancient Near East, most notably those people we now call Jews. The "New Testament" concerns the life of Christ and commentary on that life.

Christianity accepts both the "Old Testament" and the "New Testament," in the sense that Christians believe that the "Old Testament" presents the stories of those people who prepared the world, spiritually and morally, into which Christ was born. Depending on which "branch" of that faith is involved, Judaism accepts most or all of the "Old Testament." It is the basis of a Jewish person's religious and cultural history. Jews do not regard the "New Testament" as a divine document, for of course they do not accept Jesus as the Son of God, but they

17

do accept that he is a very great moral teacher and leader. Muslims (the adherents of Islam), ironically, as they are the sworn enemy of Israel and Judaism, have more in common with Judaism than with Christianity. They regard the Patriarchs — the great religious leaders described in the early books of the "Old Testament" — as founders of Islam as well. Most notably Abraham, whom they regard as the first and great leading light of Islam. As well, they regard Moses as an important spiritual leader, and revere Jesus, whom they regard as foretelling the coming of their own prophet Muhammad. Of course, given these views, neither Jews nor Muslims accepts the resurrection of Christ; indeed, they regard accounts of that event as corruptions introduced to *The Bible* by people promoting a religious agenda.

Still, the seeds of each religion, to a greater or lesser degree, are obviously all contained within this one great book. And anyone wishing to understand the modern world and its conflicts should begin by reading *The Bible,* then perhaps reading specific accounts of Christianity, Judaism and Islam to see how *The Bible* has been variously interpreted over the centuries from the time these religions were founded and how *The*

Bible became for each either the primary or a subsidiary religious guide. Part of the lesson here is that all three religions, despite occasionally painting God as wrathful or vengeful, primarily believe in a God of Love. He is not a God who asks us to destroy the Twin Towers or take revenge against its perpetrators, or, because of that revenge, plot the destruction of Israel. All three religions currently diverge from the teachings of their prophets, and reading *The Bible* shows us the extent of our misdeeds in the name of God.

Even if one has no interest in religion or in current affairs, there are still other reasons to be familiar with *The Bible.* In purely literary terms, the King James Bible is one of the world's great literary works, and, as well as the beauty of the writing contained in that translation, *The Bible,* in whatever version, contains sections — or books — acknowledged by literary scholars to be among the world's most notable literary works. The "Book of Job" is a beautifully written tragedy of loss and redemption — so fine in literary terms that it is consistently assigned in high school and college English classes. "The Psalms" are among the most beautiful lyric poems in any language. The four "Gospels" (the story of the Life of Christ) are superb novels-in-miniature. Not just the story they tell, but the way in which they tell it, has inspired writers throughout the ages. Anyone who aspires to have a well-rounded education must read *The Bible*: It is one of the greatest works of art that mankind has produced.

Yet, even supposing that a person has no interest in religion, in current events, or in literary art, there is still one more compelling reason why any person who lives in the Western world should have read *The Bible*. It is the single most important influence in the culture in which we live.

Our most important holidays are based on the stories and instructions of *The Bible;* so are the rituals we follow at birth, marriage and death. It is impossible to understand the great art of the West — not just our literary art, also our visual art — without a knowledge of *The Bible* — much of our greatest painting and sculpture is based on stories related in *The Bible.*

It is difficult — no, it is impossible — to understand the great historical conflicts in Europe, and the great explorations that led to the discoveries of the Americas and their subsequent settlement, without understanding the ways in which these events were responses to the ways in which people of the time interpreted *The Bible.* What were the Dark Ages? — why were they dark? What was the Inquisition? What was the Enlightenment? What inspired the great revolutions in America and in France? What is the Protestantism of the North of Europe — and how is it different from the Catholicism of Southern Europe?

Or, move to the modern world: Why are so many Christians agitated about prostitution or the failure of marriage or homosexuality or abortion? These moral notions are based upon the precepts of *The Bible* and the ways in which they are interpreted by various people. What does *The Bible* actually say about these and any other matters? Anyone wishing to understand the modern culture in which he or she lives should know the answer to these questions. It will interest many people to know that Jesus never mentions any of these matters — why then do so many Christians, particularly more radical Christians, feel so strongly about them? They would answer: The reasons are in *The Bible.*

Not just the modern world but so much of what has come before us, so much that mankind has done for good or bad, is based on this one book — *The Bible.*

1
HOMER:
The Iliad & The Odyssey

WHO WAS HOMER?

No precise or verifiable biographical information exists about Homer. His dates of birth and death are unknown, as are the locations where these events took place. He is believed to have lived in Ionia, subsequently a part of the Greek Empire, now the modern-day country of Turkey.

Any information that we have about Homer's personal history, background, family, education, religious beliefs, or political affiliations are pure conjecture and opinion — we have to accept that there are really no known facts about him.

All that we have are myths and legends. During the Greek and Roman eras, people took a great interest in his life because of the fame of his works. There are no fewer than 10 different accounts of his life from classical times (and probably many more that are lost to us). Each one involves contradictions of the continuities of the others and even glaring discrepancies within themselves. Some commentators believe that he was blind; others think that he was a wandering minstrel; others go so far as to claim that Homer never existed or, if he did, that he was not the author of the works that we now attribute to him.

Modern scholars believe that he did exist, that he wrote somewhere about the 8th century B.C. (the Trojan War and its aftermath, his subject, happened, if it happened at all, in the 12th century B.C.). (The references to Homer in other written works establish these dates.)

Homer's writings, *The Iliad* and *The Odyssey,* were immensely popular with the people of classical Greece; indeed, many subsequent literary works of the Greeks and Romans are based on these two epic poems. In more modern times, they have become the cornerstones of a classical education in the Western world.

THE WORKS

The Iliad & The Odyssey

No one knows who Homer really was. Yet, except for Shakespeare, more is written about Homer each year than any other writer in history. Traditionally, he was imagined to be a blind minstrel, a singer of stories who was probably a retainer in the court of one of the kings of pre-classical Greece. The first writer of the Western world whose works survive, Homer may have lived at any time between the 7th and 13th centuries B.C. Obviously, if he were blind, someone else must have written down the stories that Homer sang from memory.

Scholars of the 19th and early 20th centuries tampered with that story — Homer was not one person but, instead, he was many people who lived over many different centuries: that is, his great works, *The Iliad* and *The Odyssey,* are, like *The Bible,* the work of many hands. More recently, scholars have pointed out that diverse sections of these two works — unlike *The Bible* — are remarkably similar in both style and diction; as well, they involve well-organized plots. For these reasons most people now again accept that Homer was probably one person, that he (or she) lived in the 8th century B.C. (in other words: 4 centuries before the glory days of Athens), that he recorded and organized the stories and myths of the Greek world, that he probably did speak these myths — recite or sing them in some king's court or at public events and festivals

— and that at some point (probably long after his death), these stories were written down in something resembling the form in which they have come down to us.

Does it matter? Asking such a question is like asking: Was Shakespeare really a basically uneducated man from Stratford-upon-Avon, an itinerant actor, and did this same Shakespeare really write the greatest poetry and plays in the English language? We'll probably never be able to answer the question: "Who was Homer?" Just as we may never be able to answer the question: "Did the historical Shakespeare really write the plays that we now attribute to him?" All that finally matters are the works themselves.

The Iliad, usually translated as verse, tells the story of the Trojan War: Paris, Prince of Troy, falls in love with Helen, wife of Menelaus, king of Sparta, and abducts her to Troy. The other kings of Greece — notably Agamemnon, king of the Achaeans (the most powerful of the kings) — rally to avenge Meneleus, sail to Troy in "a thousand ships," and there wage a war that lasts for 10 years, because, despite all their efforts, the Greeks are unable to scale the walls of Troy and conquer the city. *The Iliad* happens in the 10th year of the war — the Greeks are thwarted — their greatest warrior, Achilles, refuses to fight. At last provoked to fight, Achilles kills Paris' older brother Hector, and *The Iliad* ends with Hector's funeral. From *The Odyssey* and from *The Aeneid,* the continuation of the Trojan story by Virgil, the greatest of Roman poets, we learn that, after killing Hector, Achilles is himself killed — and the remaining Greeks pretend to abandon Troy, leaving in their stead a great wooden horse, a homage to the monumental battle that the two sides have just fought. The Trojans bring the horse inside their walls. The horse is filled with a small contingent of Greeks, who, during the night, while most of Troy is sleeping, leave the horse, open the city gates, and admit the vast legions of Greek soldiers (who have only pretended to leave the area). The Greeks destroy the city and massacre Hiram, king of Troy and Paris' father.

The Odyssey, in modern times usually translated as prose, not only describes the fate of Troy; it also tells of the fates of the various kings as they return home to Greece. Yet it focuses primarily on one of those kings, Odysseus, notable for his wisdom and cunning, who, after the sack of Troy, wanders the earth for another 10 years before he is allowed by the Gods to return to his own kingdom of Ithaca. *The Odyssey* is his story and that of the wife and son who he left behind, who have lived without him for 20 years.

Both stories are epics — that is, stories of cataclysmic events rendered in exalted language. Besides Homer and Virgil, other great epic writers have been Dante (*The Divine Comedy*) and Milton (*Paradise Lost*). Most of these other notable epics have what we would call agendas — either religious or political or both. Homer is unique in merely telling the most important historical story of his people (rather as an American poet might tell objectively the story of the Civil War). In its emphasis on character and the motivations of character, *The Odyssey* is now also widely regarded as the first novel.

Did Troy actually happen? For centuries, scholars thought it was only a myth. In the early 19th century a city, now called Troy, was discovered on the western coast of Turkey. It is a city that has existed in different forms at different times — but one that was definitely destroyed (before being rebuilt) about 1200 B.C. Many scholars now feel that that is approximately the time that the war Homer was describing probably happened. Whether or not the particulars were as Homer describes them, a conflict

27

within the world of the eastern Mediter-
ranean, between those countries that we
now call Greece and Turkey, actually happened.

THE IMPORTANCE OF HOMER

Does that matter either? Not really. Homer
used the occasion of this war, whether or
not it actually happened, as a means of telling the most popular stories of his people
— and produced works of the imagination
so powerful that they have been avidly read
for thousands of years. But they have virtues
beyond the literary — and they deserve our
attention for reasons other than that they
tell stories that have enthralled people
throughout history.

They influenced the Greece that came
after Homer: virtually all of the Greek plays
that we know are variants on the themes of
Troy. Virtually all of the great philosophers
of Greece (notably those of Plato and
Aristotle) are steeped in Homeric values. As
the power of Greece faded, its place as the
dominant power in the Western world was
assumed by Rome, and Rome appropriated
all of these stories and values as its own.
Between them — their art, their philosophy,
their accomplishment in the various academic disciplines, their laws, their science

and technology — Greece and Rome have been the greatest single influence on the Western world — and in a very real sense *The Iliad* and *The Odyssey* are *The Bible* of the ancient classical world in whose shadow we still live.

Anyone wishing to understand his or her culture must understand the Greeks, the first of the Western world's great civilizations, and the clue to that understanding is in Homer. Every reader will recognize incidents, characters and especially sayings/expressions that are part of our common heritage — "The Face That Launched a Thousand Ships, A Trojan Horse, Achilles Heel and Scylla and Charybdis."

Yet it is the moral teachings of Homer that are even more important to us. The Renaissance in Europe, the awakening that ended the Middle Ages, essentially has to do with Europe's rediscovery of the Greeks, their myths in the service of their philosophy and their morality. The spirituality of Homer, combined with the tradition of Judeo-Christianity, is the heritage with which we live today. We are all the children of Homer and the world he both recorded and created. *The Bible* provides for many of us our religious faith, but *The Iliad* and *The Odyssey* offer the moral standards by

29

which men and women, on a day-to-day basis, still live.

2
CONFUCIUS:
The Analects

WHO WAS CONFUCIUS?

Much of what we know about the life of Confucius is almost certainly fiction — a good deal of it is probably legendary (his name is more often rendered in Chinese as the equivalent of Kong Fuzi or K'ung-fu, meaning Great Master Kong; Confucius is the Latinized, Western, version of his name). We think that he lived in the 6th–7th centuries before Christ (probably 551–479 B.C.), that he was born in the state of Lu in what is now Shandong Province, China. He may have married at an early age; he had one son and two daughters.

The story is also that his family, once noble, became poor; yet, despite his impoverished early life, he rose to positions in China of great prominence. More certain — we know these facts from his writings — is that he was a thinker, a philosopher, possibly a political figure, an educator, and the founder of what is now called the Ru school of Chinese thought.

What is without question is the position that he holds in the history of Chinese thought. In much of the Western world, Jesus is regarded as the great spiritual and religious teacher; Socrates, as conveyed to us by Plato, is the great philosopher-moralist, the person in the West who has been most influential in describing how a man should live his life — in society, in this world. Confucius has had the same influence in the Far East. He is the Socrates of China.

THE WORKS

The Analects

As the "dialogues" of Plato provide us with the thought of Socrates, so do what we now call *The Analects* give us the thought of Confucius (*The Analects* are probably his writings and sayings, collected by his followers after his death). The subjects of his thought are these: The proper education of a man; how he should behave — that is, how he should act not just on his own but in his interactions with others; the form of government that is ideal — that which a ruler should strive for.

Put another way: Confucius can be said

to have three topics: 1) How a man should be educated; 2) how he should behave in society; and 3) how he should govern others.

Education

Confucius emphasizes the importance of education, but it is education that is anything but passive: he does not believe in any kind of schooling that involves just study. Yes, real study does involve finding a good teacher, imitating that person, listening to what he says and recommends. But equally important is reflecting on what one has learned. In other words: Confucius would disapprove of that modern student who does nothing but write down on a pad what his professor has said in a lecture. Instead, he recommends reflection. He says: "He who studies but does not also think is lost." Education, then, as we might say, is an interactive process. Confucius as well talks about "six arts," or "six subjects," that are important in education, but he obviously regards morality (how we behave) as the most important subject for study.

His teaching methods are also interesting. He believes that a teacher should pose questions, cause students to understand the classic works of history — but his most important directive is that students should participate — with the teacher — in the learning process. His goal, as a teacher, is to create gentlemen in the old-fashioned sense — people who have poise, who speak correctly, but who — this is the most important result — behave with integrity in all aspects of life. The purpose of education, in other words, is that students learn to be virtuous.

Behavior

Confucius believes that certain limits on man are imposed by both his creator and by nature itself. Yet, within these boundaries, men are responsible for their actions and, particularly, for their treatment of others. This is a philosophy not very different from one that says: God creates the world; Nature imposes limits; but both God and Nature then leave man to fend for himself. How he "fends" is supremely important to Confucius. We can do nothing to change our fate in such matters as our "allotted time" on earth — but we ourselves are responsible for what we accomplish; we are responsible, too, for how others remember us.

This philosophy of behavior has to do with the concept of ren — which means "compassion for" and "loving" others. Practicing ren often involves putting others — whether family or friends — before oneself, and such altruism can be accomplished only by those who have learned self-discipline. One should behave in a way that gains the respect and admiration of others.

Government

Confucius's ideas about who should govern and how is really an extension of his views about the ordinary individual's day-to-day behavior. A ruler should learn self-discipline, should govern his subjects (his constituents) by being himself an example of virtue, should treat those that he governs with love and concern. Even in Confucius's own time, the idea — to which we in the West now mainly subscribe — that government should be that which enforces laws — was gaining the ascendancy. Yet, Confucius believed an emphasis on "legalism" was wrong, that rulers should rule by example — that they should attempt to be more virtuous than the people they governed. So that the ruler was admired, so this admiration inspired loyalty in those he ruled, so that force of any kind was never needed.

Confucius was interested in the language of the governor, the name that he and others used to describe himself, the process by which a governor was constantly attempting to "rectify," to adjust his behavior to make it correspond to the grandeur of the name. A modern example would be the presidency of the United States. Any president — could Confucius comment upon the modern presidency — must strive to live up to the best of that office, not the worst; any president must constantly "work on" (rectify) himself to achieve an ideal of the presidency.

None of these ideas seem foreign to a western reader. Confucius's notions of education are similar to our own notions of what a classical education ought to accomplish. His notions of behavior sound like a variant of the Golden Rule. His ideas about government remind us of Plato's ideas of what a philosopher-king can accomplish — or Shakespeare's notions of what an ideal ruler should be. We can say that they add up to a kind of virtuous humanism, and, in so saying, realize, from reading *The Analects,* that perhaps not so much separates East and West as previously we may have thought.

3
AESCHYLUS:
The Oresteia

WHO WAS AESCHYLUS?

Aeschylus (525–456 B.C.) was the earliest and the greatest of the three major play-wrights of Ancient Greece: the other two are Sophocles and Euripides. Little is known for certain about his life, little that is not legend: tradition says that he was born into a prominent family in Eleusis, near Athens. We know that he fought at the battle of Marathon (against the Persians — the great victory in Greek history), and that he won several prizes for his plays. He wrote more than 70 plays, yet only a handful survive; of these the most famous are *Agamemnon, The Libation Bearers,* and the *Eumenides,* which together comprise the trilogy *Oresteia.* The trilogy is arguably the greatest play to come to us from Ancient Greece — and it is generally regarded, as well, as one of the great works of world literature.

Aeschylus is credited with the invention of tragedy. It could be argued that one of his predecessors (someone we don't know, someone whose works are lost) could well be responsible. The simple fact is that we have none of these predecessors' works and that, for us, tragedy therefore begins with Aeschylus. What is more certain is that he introduced to drama what we now take for granted — the addition of a second character to dramatic scenes. Formerly, in Greek plays, the action that took place involved a single actor and a chorus of commentators. These are great accomplishments, to be sure, but Aeschylus is perhaps even more notable as a "thinker," a playwright who introduced his audiences to notions that still resound with us 25 centuries later.

THE WORKS

The Oresteia

The Orestia involves a plot that originates with Homer; it was almost certainly embellished by those writer/composers of epics who came after Homer (most of whose works are unknown to us). It is the story of the House of Atreus.

That story is this: Atreus and Thyestes, the sons of the former king of Argos, were in dispute; Atreus claimed the throne;

Thyestes not only disputed his claim, but had as well seduced his brother's wife. Thyestes lost the battle between them, was banished, yet returned years later, with his children, to beg forgiveness. Pretending to be reconciled, Atreus invited Thyestes to a feast. He killed all of Thyestes's children but one, served them as the main course at the feast, and Thyestes ate the flesh of his own dead children. Thyestes put his curse on his brother's house, and fled with his surviving son, Aegisthus. The sons of Atreus, Agamemnon and Menelaus, eventually inherited the kingdom of Argos, and married, respectively, Clytaemestra and Helen, who were themselves sisters. Clytaemestra and Agamemnon had three children — Iphigeneia, Electra, and Orestes. Paris, one of the princes of Troy, seduced Helen, took her back to Troy, and the brothers vowed revenge. They convinced the other kings of Greece to join them in the destruction of Troy, and the "1,000 ships" of the Greek kings gathered for the voyage to Troy at Aulis, where they were held by wind and weather — until Agamemnon, told by his seer to do so, sacrificed his daughter, Iphigeneia. The fleet was then allowed to set sail for Troy.

In the 10th year of battle the Greeks

captured and destroyed the city and enslaved those of its people they did not kill.
On the way back to Greece, the Greeks
encountered a great storm at sea, and all
their ships were sunk or lost to sight
(subsequently, in other Greek stories, we
learn that some of the ships survived — for
example, those of Odysseus). Agamemnon
returned to Argos with a single ship, carry-
ing not only what remained of his troops
but also enslaved Trojans and, as well, Cas-
sandra, princess of Troy, who had become
his mistress. It is at this point that the play
Agamemnon begins.

Aegisthus, now a man, has seduced Clytaemestra. The lovers now rule Argos as
dictators, Clytaemestra having banished Orestes, who has vehemently opposed his
mother's actions; his sister Electra, powerless, remains in Argos. Clytaemestra, waiting until her unsuspecting husband is
unarmed and in his bath, stabs Agamemnon to death, then, as well, murders Cas-
sandra. Because of the power of the despots,
their subjects acquiesce, accept them as
legitimate rulers.

In *The Libation Bearers,* which takes place
many years after the close of *Agamemnon,*
Orestes returns, disguised as a traveler
bringing news of his own death, makes

contact with Electra, and together they plan to avenge their father. Orestes gains access to the palace and kills his mother and her lover. He believes that the cycle of bloodshed is at an end, but that is not possible; his view is hopelessly optimistic. Almost immediately, the Furies (also called *Eumenides*), which are really symbols of society's demand for retribution for his murder of his mother, appear to him, torment him, drive him out of Argos. He takes refuge with Apollo, the God of the arts and intellect (Apollo symbolizes the best that human beings can attain), who purifies him.

In *The Eumenidies,* Orestes, still pursued by the Furies, is referred to Athens and to its patroness, the greatest (after Zeus himself) of the divinities, Athena, goddess of wisdom and justice. The Furies argue for Orestes's destruction; Apollo argues for his acquittal. Athena, reserving to herself any deciding vote, refers the matter to what we would call a "jury," a group of mortal men. Their vote is tied, and Athena casts the deciding vote in Orestes's favor, and placates the Furies by placing them in a new role, minor gods in Athens. With this episode, *The Oresteia* ends.

It is necessary to stand back from the great panorama of *The Oresteia* and consider what it means. Aeschylus is considering the moral code, the legal code, of the ancient Greek world — which is not so different from that of the ancient world we know from *The Bible;* an eye for an eye, a ceaseless cycle of vengeance in the name of justice. The single most obvious fact of the story of the House of Atreus is that it is a story of never-ending revenge: Atreus kills the children of Thyestes except for Aegisthus; Aegisthus, avenging his father and his siblings, with Clytaemestra, who is avenging the death of her daughter Iphigeneia, kills the son of Atreus, Agamemnon; Orestes, the son of Agamemnon, with his sister, plot the death of, then kill, their mother — as revenge for their father's death; then the Furies taunt Orestes for his crime, pursue him until they can destroy him. In the background the Trojan War looms — which in itself is a lesson in revenge begetting revenge begetting revenge, ending in not only the destruction of Troy but, as well, that of most of the young men of Greece, the victors. In these stories, violence never ends, no one ever wins.

Finally, the matter — this case, which involves not just Orestes but is also the story of what passes for "justice" in Ancient Greece — the never-ending cycle of retribution — is referred to Athena, the symbol to the Greeks of an eternal wisdom to which no individual mortal may aspire. Athena says and does two things; in effect, she says: The Furies are always with us — the barbarous inclination of man cannot be destroyed; it exists, and exists forever. Man cannot become Apollo — he may aspire to be, but the Furies arc part of his nature. They must be recognized as such, given the status of minor gods — acknowledged to be part of human nature, just as Apollo, the god of man at his best, is part of our mortal nature. Yet, the civilized will triumph over the barbarous (Apollo will win over the Furies) only if man agrees to laws in the ultimate service of the good — and shows that agreement by accepting the decision of mortal "juries" in matters such as the saga of the House of Atreus. Only by the rule of law can the Furies in us be kept at bay and the Apollo in us cultivated — because the law is in the service of Athena (wisdom) herself.

Aeschylus has, in The *Oresteia,* offered notions that, though he could not have known their effect, would change the world — that the sins of man are eternal, that they can be controlled, that we can strive for virtue but only if virtue is enshrined in laws, laws that ensure the greatest possible good, laws that are administered by man on behalf of man.

4
HERODOTUS:
The Histories

WHO WAS HERODOTUS?

Herodotus — sometimes called Herodotus of Halicarnassus, after the city where he was born — lived during the 5th century B.C. (484–424 B.C.), the "glory days" of Ancient Greece, and we know more about his life than we do about many of the lives of his famous contemporaries, possibly because, strictly speaking, he wasn't really Greek at all. Halicarnassus is a city of Asia Minor, now Bodrum in southwestern Turkey: during his lifetime it was part of the Persian, not the Greek, empire. But Herodotus, it seems, wished to be Greek, the dominant "intellectual" power of the time. After his exile from Halicarnassus (he had been involved in an unsuccessful attempt to depose its rulers), he spent most of his life traveling throughout the Greek Empire, recording what he saw of daily life. Most notably, recording the great battles between the two empires, which finally involved the triumph of the Greeks over the Persians, a triumph that made the Greeks the dominant power in the Western world.

THE WORKS

The Histories

Herodotus's monumental work concerns the rise of the Persian Empire, the Persian invasions of Greece in 490 and 480 B.C., and the Greek's battles with and final victory over the Persian Empire, which made the Greeks the dominant power in the Western world. For this achievement, he has been called the "Father of History."

Isn't Homer equally deserving of the title? True, Homer recorded not contemporary events, but he did compose epics about momentous events that had transpired centuries before his time. Or, couldn't the same things be said about the great playwrights who borrowed Homer's stories and those of the epic writers who came after him, adding their own embellishments, to create the great Greek tragedies? The accomplishment of Herodotus is very different from those of these other men, however notable their accomplishments may have been.

Homer, and the great playwrights who

came after him, were, in reality, recycling the great legends and myths of their people, much as Shakespeare did many centuries later. In reading Homer and later scribes, we must ask ourselves: Was there really a Trojan War? Did the Greeks defeat the Trojans and destroy Trojan civilization? Did the Trojans, as the great Roman poet Virgil claimed in *The Aeneid,* really go on to found the Roman Empire? Such questions are similar to those we might ask about Shakespeare: Did Hamlet, Prince of Denmark, really exist? Did he try to avenge his father? Was there a medieval king of Scotland called Macbeth whose wife spurred him to murderous acts in an attempt to gain the crown? Such questions merely beg other questions: What in our literature, and the literature of the ancients, is really fact? What is fiction? Will we ever know the answer to such questions? Probably not.

Herodotus is very different. He called what he produced "historie," meaning, in his own time and in his own language, an "inquiry." The word passed into the Latin of the Romans and came to mean a "story" — in our sense of the word "history." It was 3 centuries later that the great Roman writer Cicero referred to Herodotus as the "Father of History."

What, precisely, did Cicero mean? He was referring to what had passed for "history" before Herodotus began to write — for example, that Paris had abducted Helen, the wife of a Greek king, that the Greeks had avenged this insult by sailing in their 1,000 ships to Troy, then battling Troy for 10 years until they had defeated that kingdom, which battle in turn gives us the story of Agamemnon and Achilles and Odysseus. These stories may or may not be true. Herodotus, very differently, was trying to record what he actually saw in his travels and what he actually knew of the actual events of contemporary Greek life and the immediate past history of the Greeks.

To modern readers that difference is hard to grasp — simply because we take such a difference for granted. If we read a novel, we know that the plot of the novel is the invention of the novelist, even though it may involve a certain kind of "truth" — yes, we might say: this story is contrived by the novelist, yet this novelist's rendering of his characters is consistent with what we know about people of that kind. But if we read an account of current or past events — a conflict or any event in which our country is or was involved or other countries are or were involved — if we read it in a newspaper or magazine, see it portrayed on television or on the Internet, or read it in a book that claims to be "history" — we expect that all particulars are true, not "made up," even if we make allowances for media distortions.

Herotodus was striving for the latter kind of truth, as distinct from all of his predecessors, who were striving for the former kind of truth, and, for this reason, he deserves Cicero's compliment, that he invented history as we know it.

It is ironic that Herodotus was taken at his own word, then doubted. Even in antiquity, many commentators questioned whether Herodotus had really traveled to as many parts of the Greek Empire as he said that he did after his exile, questioned too some of his assumptions and claims about events in Greece's immediate past. This "questioning" persisted almost to modern times. More recent discoveries (from the beginning of, and throughout, the 20th century) have served to prove that, in most of his pronouncements, Herodotus was telling the truth or had done his homework, was presenting, as near as possible, the real record of his times.

The body of his work is known as *The Histories,* and these works were published between 430 B.C. and 424 B.C. — within the space of 6 years, in other words. Later editors divided his work into nine books. All of them, besides offering observations gleaned from his travels, document the growth of the Persian Empire, its defeat at Marathon, its attempt to avenge that defeat, 10 years later, by absorbing Greece into its empire, leading to its eventual defeat, in 479 B.C., at the Battle of Plataea.

In 431 B.C., the Polyponnesian War broke out — between the two main kingdoms of Greece, Athens and Sparta. Herodotus may have been provoked to publish his works, beginning the year after — to inspire Greece not to destroy itself in a Civil War, by reminding his readers of the glory days of the empire, when they had defeated the seemingly invincible Persian Empire.

In this goal, too, he seems like a modern man — as, say, a contemporary American historian might write about World War II as a wake-up call to modern America, to remind it of the sacrifice of that time, its people coming together, forgetting their differences, in a noble effort to defeat oppressors and free the world's peoples — as to way of inspiring America to be at its best again.

For the beginnings of history as a discipline, and to understand how the profession came to be, and to understand what historians try to accomplish — as well as to be given a glimpse of what the ancient Greek world was really like — any informed reader will want to have sampled the *Histories* of Herodotus.

5

PLATO:
The Republic

WHO WAS PLATO?

Everyone knows Plato, or at the very least, knows of him. Of course we also know of Pericles of Athens or Nero of Rome, as well as many other people of the ancient worlds of Greece and Rome whose fame continues to the present day — Aristotle or Cicero, Sophocles or Virgil. They are as much a part of our history as are the great figures of the Jewish/Christian world. But, among the well-known "stars" of the Greek and Roman worlds, Plato is by far the most famous.

Most of us know at least a few facts about him — that he was born into a well-to-do family and lived in Athens, the greatest of Greek cities, in the 4th century B.C. (he lived from 427 to 347 B.C.); that he was a student of the great teacher, Socrates; that at the age of 40 he founded the Academy, one of the most renowned schools in history; and that he continued to teach at the

Academy for the rest of his life, where he was the teacher of Aristotle, one of the pre-eminent philosophers in human history. Some of us may also know that Plato was himself a great philosopher. One of his best-known philosophers of more recent times has said: "All subsequent philosophy is a footnote to Plato." In other words, there is a very strong case for regarding Plato as the father of philosophy, if not its greatest practitioner. Literary scholars might add: Plato was one of the greatest creative writers who ever lived.

THE WORKS

The Republic

Plato was obviously the most prominent teacher at the Academy he founded, but his lectures notes, like those of most illustrious teachers from the past, have not survived. What we have instead is his writings. All of his thought is there, rendered in such a way that we must admit: this is not cold philosophical theory presented in textbook form; this is first and foremost a series of dramatic stories that are truly excellent of their kind. His writings do, however, also convey what Plato regarded as philosophical truths — much as Jesus conveyed what he regarded as the certainties of human life and eternity via the literary device of parables. One of the generally accepted facts about Plato is that he started out as a playwright — and he was obviously a skillful one — he conveys his philosophy through the devices of the drama (setting, characters, conflict). One of the facts/legends about Plato was that he was inspired to change from drama to philosophy as a result of Socrates's influence on his early life.

Yet, most of us, nowadays, do not experience what used to be called a "classical education." It is very likely that most of us (unlike people before the advent of the modern world) have not read the ancient writers and philosophers: we know Plato only by reputation.

His greatest works are "dialogues" ("plays," we might call them), a form that he employed for all of his life. In them, his hero, Socrates, is found in a variety of situations — lecturing his disciples in a public forum or meeting with them, for conversation, at a dinner party or strolling with friends outside the walls of Athens. All the evidence is that Socrates actually lived, that he was a kind of itinerant teacher (unconnected with any formal "institution"), that he was put to death (by being forced to drink hemlock) for "impiety" (not accepting the received religion of the time) and for "corrupting" the youth of Athens — giving them notions of which the government of Athens disapproved. So much we know. But whether he actually thought and said everything that Plato attributes to him is open to dispute. Because Socrates, unlike Plato, was not also a writer, we can only conjecture what, in Plato, about Socrates, is real and what is not. Most scholars feel that the early dialogues of Plato, following the death of Socrates (he died in 399 B.C.; Plato was then about 30 years old) are fairly accurate transcriptions of what Socrates thought and said. As Plato continued writing, as he got further and further away from the time of Socrates's death, he more or less becomes his own man. The dialogues increasingly become reflections of his own thought, even though Socrates continues to be his hero, even though Plato's thoughts continue to be attributed to Socrates (as a character, he is missing from only Plato's last work, *Laws*).

What exactly did Socrates have to say? His thought is so complex, involves so many ruminations on human life, that it is perhaps best to make a few generalizations. In the Western world, our notions of the divine, of the condition and nature of God, are those of the great Jewish thinkers (if we are Jews), Jesus Christ (if we are Christians), or Muhammad (if we are Muslim). Our notions of morality — of what is right and wrong in human behavior, of what our intellectual goals as men and women should be — are all traceable to Socrates — as he is created for us by Plato. Socrates says: The proper pursuit of men should be refinement of the intellect, so that we are able to see the "truth" in life, so that we are able to behave in our own lives (or in our interactions with others) according to the truths we gain. Yet Socrates, in offering these notions, says, I myself know nothing; I merely ask constant questions.

The search for truth (which is also the ultimate in "beauty") is a life-long pursuit — just as, say, the search for grace, for pleasing God, is a lifelong pursuit in Christianity. We come to Socratic truth by a constant searching of our assumptions, by admitting when we are wrong, by admitting too that we are more often wrong than right — and do so via the device of conversing and testing our assumptions with like-minded companions. It is only gradually that we come to truth. "The unexamined life is not worth living," said Socrates; our notions, even those ideas we already regard as true, must be constantly re-examined, constantly challenged.

Any of Plato's dialogues will provide the reader with a sense of what Plato and his hero, Socrates, were preaching: any one will serve to demonstrate the method of constant questioning of assumptions to arrive at larger, abiding truths. But *The Republic* is probably the most profound of all of Plato's works.

In *The Republic* (probably written about 390 B.C.), Plato most clearly defines what he has been driving at all along. Here he offers his belief in "forms," that there exists, in the universe, a perfect example of anything we know, from our senses, on earth — a universal. The ultimate of these is the Form of the Good (in effect, Plato's God). We strive, in human life, to know what unchanging perfection would be like, but we see these universals only dimly, if at all, because we know the world only through our senses, not through our minds. Those "dim glimpses" become less dim, more real to us, the greater the refinement of our mind, our intellect and our understanding. For example (to take a simple example): a table. All tables we create, in human life, are attempts to emulate the "form" of the universal table, and we strive, with each table we create, to get nearer to the perfect table. Of course, what Plato is most concerned about is what we would call abstractions: what is courage, what is sincerity, what, finally, is perfect love? *The Republic* is Plato's most vivid rendering of what he regards as the most important goal in human life — to bring ourselves closer and closer, through self-knowledge, to these elusive "forms" of perfection. This is the ultimate virtue, and this is the activity that Plato recommends as a means for human beings to "live well."

But *The Republic* is something more. Plato is also examining the institutions we create as a result of self-knowledge, and his interest is in the most important of human institutions — the ways in which we choose to govern ourselves. Those who have achieved the greatest knowledge — the "philosopher king" is an expression that has entered our language — those who are, in other words, most like Socrates — are those who should rule. They are disinterested persons who rule not for their personal benefit but for the good of everyone else — in them, the gift for ruling, for the exercise of power, and the gift for philosophy, for the exercise of thought about perfection in human behavior, entirely coincide. Just as the most advanced person should run a family, or the most advanced person should be the principal of a school, or the most gifted executive should run a company.

Of course, Plato, in *The Republic,* in all of the dialogues, is talking about ideals, ideals of conduct, or ideals of intellectual inquiry, or ideals of government — they remain always out of our reach. Raise that objection, and Plato would respond: The striving for that goal of perfection is the business of human life; there is no other, whether you succeed or not — and you will not ultimately succeed. The striving is everything, the distance you move your greatest reward.

We should all be aware of the ideals of *The Republic* — and these goals — which 2,500 years later are still, if we are honest, our most precious goals, that for which, in our best moments, all human beings still strive.

6
ARISTOTLE:
Metaphysics

WHO WAS ARISTOTLE?

Aristotle is one of the most famous men who ever lived. Everyone knows his name, and, unlike many of the most prominent of the ancient Greeks, we know the facts of his life — most are documented, few are legend. After a childhood in Macedonia (he was born in 384, died in 322 B.C.), where his father was the court physician, Aristotle, at age 18, went to Athens to study with Plato at Plato's Academy. He remained there until Plato's death in 347 when he was himself 37 years old. Passed over as Plato's successor (this happened twice in his lifetime), Aristotle traveled, eventually arriving at the court of Philip of Macedonia, where he became tutor to young Alexander the Great (when Alexander was 13 years old). He remained Alexander's tutor for 5 years, until Alexander was a man and had himself ascended the throne of Macedonia and went off on his campaigns of conquest in Asia.

At that point, Aristotle returned to Athens, founded the Lyceum (a school in the style of Plato's Academy), and from then until his early death at the age of 62, he continued to teach and to do most of the writing for which we now remember him. Ironically, his work was not published in his lifetime. It languished in one of the great libraries of Athens until the 1st century B.C. when Athens was sacked, and its treasures taken back to Rome — where Aristotle's works were at last published. As a result of that publication, his fame spread to all corners of the Roman Empire.

THE WORKS

Metaphysics

Everyone is aware that Aristotle was a great philosopher. But that is not the entire story. With Plato, he is now regarded as one of the two greatest philosophers produced by ancient Greece. But there is even more to his accomplishment than that — Plato can be said to have created the Idealistic School of philosophy; Aristotle is credited with creating the Empirical School of Philosophy — distinctions in philosophy that persist until this day. Plato's reputation went into a decline (it has recovered in modern times);

Aristotle's views dominated Western thought for more than 15 centuries. Aristotle's thought was the only accepted thought for longer than any other thinker has ever held sway in the history of the Western world. His influence, obviously, has now waned.

Aristotle spent only 13 years at the Lyceum, but his writings were voluminous. Aristotle did not understand the "term" philosopher in quite the same way that we do — as someone who studies human knowledge and develops systems for understanding human experience. Aristotle, almost certainly, thought of himself as what we mean by a scientist, someone who examines the facts and laws of the physical world and tries to understand the workings of nature as a way to develop the facility of human reasoning. He studied, and wrote about, virtually every subject that existed in his time — from anatomy to geography, from geology to zoology. Unlike Plato, he did not write imaginative literature. Most of his writings are almost certainly lecture notes and treatises created for the consumption of his students (what we might call "textbooks"); they were probably "organized" by his students after his death and by scholars and editors of later generations. As it is neither imaginative nor, initially, written for publication, Aristotle's writings can be tough going for the modern reader. Yet, it is fair to say that, in the breath of his writing, Aristotle virtually created an encyclopedia of what was known, and what was surmised, by the ancient Greeks.

Why read him if his influence has largely waned? Yes, it has waned — in the sense that Aristotle is no longer regarded by modern readers as the repository of all knowledge. But his reliance on empiricism — hypothesis offered, then tested as to its reliability, whether it holds true in experiments — remains the basis, more than 2,000 years after his death, of modern scientific method. And he continues to be influential in other ways — one of the most persistent schools of modern literary scholarship, for example, is based on principles of composition set out by Aristotle in his *Poetics* — and literary scholars still refer to the Aristotelian "unities" of time, place, incident in discussing not just the drama (his immediate subject) but other forms of literary composition. And to cite another example: In our behavior, in our ethics, we still refer to the Aristotelian "mean," meaning a life that is lived in the avoidance of excess, striving for balance and the middle way (for example: Boastfulness and bashfulness are both excesses; the goal is modest self-confidence).

So many of Aristotle's writings remain influential that it is difficult to choose one on which the modern reader should focus — but perhaps *Metaphysics* would provide an appropriate introduction. Again, it is important to understand — despite modern connotations of the word "metaphysics" — just what Aristotle was talking about. He means "after physics," and by "physics" he means the observable world. In other words: What conclusions do we reach about life after we have observed its physical manifestations? What conclusions do we reach about the meaning of life? In these concerns — indeed, in all of his philosophical writings — he differs from his mentor. Simply: Plato strived to understand universal ideals — for example, truth, justice, courage, love — and from his conclusions to extrapolate about human life; Aristotle, conversely, closely observes both human life and the natural world in which it exists, and from his conclusions about human activity and motivation attempts to construct ideals. His *Metaphysics,* then, has to do with his conclusions about "meaning," after he has long observed the world of man, not the world of ideals.

In *Metaphysics,* he asks: What are the essential attributes of man's existence, his being — are there, in other words, universal truths about man's existence that can be known?

Obviously, he believes the answer to this question is yes. He argues, too, that true being, our selfhood, is not an abstraction; it is concrete, it exists in this world. Put another way: He asks himself — and asks us to consider — what is the final end for which some aspect of life is created? What causes it to happen? What is its final purpose?

Aristotle, in short, is no longer the "be all and end all" of Western thought, yet his thought remains potent to this day, part of our mental equipment whether we know it or not. The questions he asks, in the *Metaphysics* and elsewhere, are questions we are all still asking.

7
MAHABHARATA

THE WORKS
Mahabharata

Most people in the Western world are aware
of at one time or another having heard of
the *Mahabharata* or of having read about it
in some history or literary text, but most of
us could not actually define what it is. Or
even how to pronounce it. It is Ma-ha-barr-
a-ta, with emphasis on the third syllable.

The *Mahabharata* is one of the two major
Sanskrit epics of India. It is, as well, one of
the longest epic poems in the world; it is
about 2.5 million words long. Although it is
traditionally ascribed to the ancient sage
Vyasa, also a character in the story, it is one
of those ancient works, probably begun
about 500 B.C., that tells popular and
legendary stories of Gods and kings and
their adventures, and it is almost certainly
the work of many hands — from writers to
priests to minstrels to actors. Later, in the

4th century A.D., it came to be a unified text, written down in Sanskrit. With the *Ramayana,* it constitutes the cultural memory of the Indian people, much as Homer was the cultural memory, the history and tradition, of the Greeks. Yet even though it is now more than 2,000 years old, it still exerts enormous cultural influence throughout India and Southeast Asia.

A full reading of the *Mahabharta* is probably daunting to most modern readers; it is, after all, a very long work. But there are a few compelling reasons for any reader to have sampled it:

It is, like the works of Homer, a powerful and compelling tale. It presents a sweeping panorama that includes Indian ideas of both the cosmos and of humanity and of the divinities that are part of Indian culture. It is, too, one of those works so ambitious in its storytelling and in its definitions of the life and history of humanity that it seems to transcend its time and place — much as *The Bible,* the Greek tragedies, the *Iliad* and the *Odyssey* and the works of Shakespeare transcend theirs; it is one of the comparatively few literary works produced by mankind that can be said to be "eternal." To sample it is to understand something of the culture of a vast world that is not our own.

Though, in some ways, it will seem familiar to Western readers, who know that our literature starts with the Greeks and Romans. In its mixture of the divine and the secular, in its dazzling and fantastic plot, relieved by moments of poignant encounters between mortal individuals, it reminds us of the works of Homer and Virgil.

The central story of the work is that of a dynastic struggle — and great war — for the throne of the kingdom of Hastinapura. Two collateral branches of the family participate in the struggle: the Kauravas and the Pandavas. It is a struggle (attended by Gods on both sides) that is not unlike the struggle of the sons of Argos and the sons of Troy, in the Trojan War, for the soul of Greece.

Much will seem familiar to the reader — not least the character of Krishna, a participant in the battle, who is yet a son of God, born to a mortal woman. Later in the story, he returns to heaven to be united with God.

The *Mahabharata,* in other words, is also a religious work. Besides being one of the literary triumphs of mankind, it is also a core text of the Hindu religion — one of the great religions of the world and one about which most Westerners know virtually nothing.

If readers read nothing else, they should read one of its chapters, the "Bhagavad Gita," which puts forth, in concise terms, the basic principles of Hinduism.

The *Mahabharata* is, like most of the world's great literary works, concerned about how a man should live — his values, his morality. Just as in Greek literature, the Trojan War is seen not to have accomplished anything but death, destruction and chaos, which in their wake beg all sorts of questions, so in the *Mahabharata* the cessation of the great battle is only a kind of prelude to the overwhelming moral questions that follow. In a sense, the resolution of the war is to no one's satisfaction — all anyone is left with is a sense of futility and horror.

The characters, troubled by what has happened, seek meaning — either by trying to find justification for what has happened on a grand scale or by coming themselves to some sort of inner peace, living ascetic, quiet lives. A central character, Yudhishthira, tries both ways — trying to find some justification for what has happened, at the same time that, assured by good counselors that the war was just and necessary, he searches to find personal equilibrium. The *Mahabharata* ends charmingly: Yudhishthira arrives at the gates of heaven with his dog

— he refuses to leave the dog behind, and the dog is revealed to be a god. Then, in a final test, he is told that his brothers are not in heaven but in hell, and he insists on joining them there. This, too, is revealed to be an illusion — and a test for him — his brothers are really in heaven with him.

For all of its battles and bloodshed, the *Mahabharata* ends on a quieter note, one of all-encompassing love. The *Mahabharata* provides an insight into one of the great civilizations of the East, a civilization that is growing increasingly important in world affairs — and an insight into that civilization's religion and philosophy. Yet, ironically, it shows us, in its main and abiding emphasis, that it upholds values with which we are familiar from our own literature, from its beginnings to the present, and from our own religion. If it is both the Indian *Bible* and the Indian Homer, it is not so unfamiliar to us as we might suppose and provides us with a reminder that the greatest literary minds — of whatever time and whatever part of the world — have come to many of the same religious and ethical conclusions as has our own civilization.

8
EUCLID OF ALEXANDRIA:
The Elements

WHO WAS EUCLID OF ALEXANDRIA?

So little is known of Euclid the mathematician that he is always referred to as Euclid of Alexandria to differentiate him from Euclid of Megara, a Socratic philosopher who lived roughly a century earlier. We know a few facts about Euclid of Alexandria, that he was born about 325 B.C., which means that he was born about 22 years after the death of Plato, 3 years before the death of Aristotle. In other words, he lived during the time of Plato's immediate successors, and there is some evidence that he studied at Plato's Academy in Athens. He spent most of his life in Alexandria, in Egypt, during the reign of Ptolemy I (though Egypt was then not so much the great civilization that it had once been as it was a part of the Greek Empire, a Hellenistic state. He probably worked at the great library in Alexandria (the greatest library of

71

antiquity); he was probably head of his own school of mathematics there (at least, he was the leader of a team of notable mathematicians and the students who attended them as acolytes and students); and he died in Alexandria, probably about 265 B.C.

THE WORKS

The Elements

What is extraordinary about his obscurity is that Euclid of Alexandria wrote the most famous work of antiquity on the subject of mathematics — indeed, *The Elements,* a comprehensive 13-volume work, became the standard for work in mathematics, particularly geometry, for more than 2,000 years until it began to be supplanted by non-Euclidian geometry in the 19th century. More than that, having endured for those 2,000 years, *The Elements* could be said to be the most famous textbook ever written. Some scholars have estimated that only *The Bible* has gone through more editions and more translations. *The Elements* was known to mathematicians in all times and in virtually all the civilized countries of the world. Given the prominence of this textbook over 2 millennia, Euclid of Alexandria can be said to be the most famous teacher of mathematics that the world has ever known.

Its composition is something of a mystery. Was Euclid an historical figure who single-handedly composed *The Elements* and the other works that have been attributed to him? Or was he the leader of a group of mathematicians, working under his supervision, very possibly teachers and students at his school, or scholars who had gathered around him, who "published" under his name — and continued doing so even after his death? Or did he never exist at all? Is Euclid of Alexandria simply a pseudonym for a group of mathematicians, based in Alexandria, connected to its library (a kind of university in antiquity) who took the name Euclid because it was a popular name of the time?

No one knows the answer for sure, but most scholars would now say that Euclid of Alexandria existed; that he brought together all known mathematical knowledge of the time; that he set it out in comprehensible terms that others, for centuries after his death could follow; and that he was aided in the enormous task of compiling *The Elements* by trusted fellow mathematicians, students, scholars and editors — the intellectual class that was attracted to Alexander

73

and its reputation for research and scholarship.

Very few readers, especially non-mathematicians, or non-historians of antiquity, non-classicists, are likely now to plow through and absorb all 13 volumes of Euclid's *Elements*. But most people who wish to understand human intellectual history should at least do a sampling of this mighty work, to see what it accomplished as a work of synthesis.

Most of us acknowledge that the "beginnings" of most intellectual disciplines come to us from the Greek World. Euclid is not an original thinker; rather he is a compiler, one of the greatest who ever lived. That is, Euclid did not emerge out of thin air; other mathematicians of note had preceded him. He took their work, proved that it was correct or showed that it had to be modified to be proved. In all of this, he could be said to be a Platonist; that is, he wished to show that certain "forms" were eternal, were subject to rules that could in fact be demonstrated to be true. In a sense, he was also an Aristotelian — believing that we could come to "universals" via our precise observation of and experimentation with the observable phenomena of the known world.

The accomplishment of *The Elements* is

that, within this work, Euclid describes the properties of geometrical objects, which he deduces from a relatively narrow set of axioms. He thereby defines, anticipates, and inspires the axiomatic method of modern mathematics. The book is best known for its comments on geometry, but it as well includes various conclusions about the theory of numbers — for example, the connection between perfect numbers. Yes, some of his results originate with earlier mathematicians (in some cases we don't even know who they were), but his great triumph was to present them in a single framework that made sense to those who read it — his contemporaries and those who came after him, those who studied mathematics for the next 2,000 years.

Even to non-mathematicians — to those who will never make the entire journey through *The Elements* — Euclid of Alexandria provides an example of the kind of thought that we inherited from the Greeks, that guides our studies — and our attempts to reason — even now. It was well worth any reader's taking the time to sample Euclid of Alexandria's intellectual rigor, to allow it to become, as it should be, an inspiration.

9
CICERO:
On the Good Life

WHO WAS CICERO?

Marcus Tullius Cicero (106–43 B.C.) was an orator and statesman of ancient Rome; he was, as well, one of the most influential writers in Latin literature as well as the greatest of Roman orators. Cicero's work reflected his command of Latin, and his precision in choice of words, his attention to grammar and his skillful use of narration and prose rhythm created a standard of Latin that served as the universal language of intellectual and scientific communications for hundreds of years.

Cicero was born in Arpinum, Italy, of the well-to-do family Tullii. Because he was an excellent student, he was given the opportunity to study Roman law, which was considered to be a great honor. Nevertheless, he expanded his interests beyond the law and also studied poetry, philosophy and Greek literature.

After successfully prosecuting a corrupt former governor of Sicily, he won the approval of the Roman aristocracy. With its support, Cicero became consul, Rome's highest elected political office at the time. The lawyer had also become a politician.

It was politics, unfortunately, that hastened his downfall. The First Triumvirate of Julius Caesar, Gnaeus Pompcy and Marcus Licinius Crassus expelled Cicero from Rome in 58 B.C. because he opposed their government. He was, however, permitted to return the following year. The Second Triumvirate of Octavian (later Emperor Augustus), Marcus Aemilius Lepidus, and Mark Antony, on the other hand, refused to tolerate Cicero's opposition after he wrote the *Philippics* in which he attacked Mark Antony as ruling Rome with absolute power. In 43 B.C. this Second Triumvirate had him assassinated.

During his lifetime, Cicero was a prolific writer. He wrote more than 100 orations, several of which endorse the Republican form of government; he remained staunchly opposed to any kind of one-man rule. In later years he wrote philosophical works in which he drew heavily on the moral ideas of the Greek philosophers. These works later became an important part of the education of 18th century Europeans and Americans, including most of the writers of the American Declaration of Independence and Constitution.

THE WORKS

On the Good Life

Everyone has heard of Cicero of ancient Rome. He is so famous that we tend to call him by only his "last name," as if he were Greek, not Roman. In fact his last name wasn't Cicero but Tullius. Cicero is a nickname, derived from the Latin word for "chickpea." One of the Cicero's ancestors had a cleft in the tip of his nose, hence the nickname, which Cicero, even when he became prominent statesman, refused to change. So, we've all heard of this man, so famous that we call him by the nickname that he himself used, even though it wasn't really his name.

But why is he famous?

Most people know that Cicero lived in the most thrilling days of ancient Rome. He was born in 106 B.C. and died in 43 B.C. and it was during this time that Julius Caesar and his successors lived — the time of the Republic, moving to what would become a dictatorship by emperors. Shakespeare immortalizes this period in his plays "Antony

78

and Cleopatra" and "Julius Caesar." Cicero was one of that period's most prominent statesmen.

Even as a student Cicero was already known throughout Rome for his brilliance. Although he studied law, he was also particularly fond of great writing and absorbed the works of the great literary figures of Greece. Although Cicero's family were landed gentry rather than aristocrats, Cicero achieved a career that the vast majority of men of his social class could not. He served as a magistrate (a "quaestor") in Western Sicily; thereafter, he created a very successful law practice in Rome and enjoyed more than his share of triumphs as an advocate. Then, despite the fact that his family was neither noble nor patrician, that no Tullius had ever been a consul before him, Cicero was elected a consul of Rome, and during the year he served in office he suppressed the "Catiline Conspiracy," a plot to overthrow the Republic — which brought him even more fame. Because he was responsible for putting the conspirators to death without trial (actually, a Senate decision, but Cicero was directly responsible for making it happen), he was subsequently exiled for a year, then he came back to Rome as a hero. He supported Pompey against Caesar, then, after the assassination of Caesar, he supported the claims of Octavian, Caesar's heir, against Antony's attempts to grab power. Cicero became the voice of the Senate of Rome (in which he continued to serve) against the dictates of Antony, who was Caesar's executor. Cicero became more and more a hero of the people. Cicero, despite initially praising him, also distrusted Octavian. When Antony and Octavian reconciled, and (with Lepidus) formed the Second Triumvirate, they named Caesar as an "enemy of the state," a traitor, and he was pursued, subsequently captured, beheaded, and his head displayed in public. An ignominious end to an illustrious public life.

Yet, the fame of Cicero lived on, not so much for his part in these historic events as for his words. Even after his death, and the end of the Republic, his memory survived — not as a statesman but as a great orator and writer. Those writings were so revered that they caused him to be declared a "righteous pagan" by the early Roman Catholic Church — therefore his works were regarded as worthy of preservation. St. Augustine and other church fathers quoted liberally from Cicero — one reason why so many re-creations of his works (many of which survived only in fragments) were possible.

Despite what seems like an action-filled life, Cicero still managed to write as extensively as someone who was a professional, full-time writer. Six of his books on rhetoric and (parts of) seven of his books on philosophy have survived. Just 58 of his speeches (either as advocate or senator) survive, as do some 800 of his letters. His literary output was vast; even what survives is impressively large.

Cicero is now acknowledged to be the greatest prose stylist that Rome produced (he is also acknowledged to have been a great orator, but of course we have no way of judging that reputation except by the testimony of those who heard him speak). Students of Latin still read his work to see the Latin language at its most stylish, its most elegant — much as we might lionize the great essayists/stylists in English such as Dr. Johnson or Thomas Jefferson.

But there is something more to Cicero than just his mastery of Latin. Cicero was, in a sense, the conscience of Rome. He wrote about abstract concepts of human rights, based both on law and custom, as well drawing on the wisdom of the writers/philosophers who had preceded him, and in so doing, he often suggests various of the goals and virtues enshrined in such much later documents as the "Declaration of Independence" or "The Rights of Man." Cicero also wrote about such subjects as duty, friendship, the training of leaders, what it meant to be moral (a person of integrity), and the conditions by which a person might be happy.

We think of Greece as having established various of our intellectual disciplines — and even the concept of government for, by and of the people to which we subscribe. When we are not contemplating the Romans as world-conquerors or tyrants flinging Christians to lions, we acknowledge that it is, from them, that we inherit more modest but just as enduring values — our laws (the notion of the rule of law) and our ideas of what constitutes domestic virtue and happiness. Cicero is the prime Roman voice of such virtues — of notions of how a man should live his life. It is Cicero who is often credited with being the voice of the Italian Renaissance when it happened centuries later, when thinkers of the Renaissance turned again to the writings of ancient Greece and Rome.

Cicero never wrote a book called *On the Good Life.* It is compilation of various of his writings, compiled and translated by Michael Grant, and published in the 1970s, but it helps us to see the breadth and flavor of his writings. The "good life" for Cicero was two kinds of lives: A life of moral value and a life of contentment (of happiness), and the two were intertwined. A person cannot have contentment, in Cicero's view, unless he lives a life that is virtuous. Moral integrity, in other words, is the means to human happiness. Cicero talks of friendship, of our duty to our friends, our family, our country — and he offers a kind of extended lesson in ethics; his lesson is simple, it is universal; it is, of course, very difficult to live up to.

We should all sample and savor Cicero via this excellent anthology of his works — for Cicero espouses values that, since the time he articulated them, have never died as ethical guideposts for mankind.

10

LUCRETIUS:
De Rerum Natura (On the Nature of Things)

WHO WAS LUCRETIUS?

Lucretius (99–55 B.C.), whose full name was Titus Lucretius Carus, was a Roman poet and philosopher. His only surviving work is the epic poem *De Rerum Natura (On the Nature of Things)*.

Little is known about Lucretius's life. Because of his name, he was thought to be from the noble family of Lucretii, although it is possible that he was a former slave who had been freed by that family. His command of language and the depth of learning reflected in his work support the idea of his having been an aristocrat.

All that is certain is that he was a poet devoted to the teachings of the philosopher Epicurus, and that he evidently died before completing his epic poem. But *De Rerum Natura* itself reveals Lucretius to be not only an accomplished poet, but also a gifted philosopher, critic of religion, social commentator, and observer of culture.

Despite the obscurity of his life, Lucretius had great literary influence, especially among such poets as Virgil, John Milton and Walt Whitman. In addition to being one of the primary sources of Epicurean ideas, his work was the forerunner of Western scientific thought — he anticipated modern theories in biology, geology, sociology, and medicine. To the Spanish poet and philosopher George Santayana (1863 — 1952), for example, Lucretius was the creator of scientific materialism. Some scholars also believe that Lucretius's ideas influenced Charles Darwin, although Darwin claimed not to have read *De Rerum Natura.* One influence is certain, however, in advocating the material basis of the human mind as a collection of atoms, Lucretius prepared the groundwork for modern neuroscience and its reliance on molecular processes.

THE WORKS
De Rerum Natura
Mention Lucretius (Titus Lucretius Carus) to most educated people and, unless they are philosophers or classicists, they probably won't know whom you are talking about. Yet philosophers would say that he is

one of the most innovative and profound of the philosophers of ancient Rome. Classicists and literary scholars would say that he is one of the greatest of Roman poets — some have said that his only known work, *De Rerum Natura (On the Nature of Things* or, as sometimes translated, *On the Nature of the World/the Universe),* is greater than Virgil's "Aeneid," that it is the masterpiece of Latin verse. Even those who would not go that far would admit that *De Rerum Natura* is very important for its influence on Virgil and other of the Roman poets. Perhaps its greatest achievement is in the excellence of its verse combined with the innovation of its philosophy. Yet, to modern readers, Lucretius remains an unknown person, *De Rerum Natura* virtually an unknown work.

There are perhaps two reasons for this dual obscurity. Almost nothing is known about Lucretius — even the dates of his birth and death (possibly he lived from 99 B.C. to 55 B.C.) are conjecture, provoked by other people's references to him, particularly those of St. Jerome. Jerome claims that Lucretius lived to be age 44, that he had drunk a love potion and was insane for most of his life, writing his poem only during moments of lucidity, and that he committed suicide during a period of madness. Jerome, who would have objected to Lucretius's anti-religious stance, may well have been trying to discredit Lucretius. It is hardly possible that a lunatic could have composed a poetic masterpiece; besides, a rather engaging and rational personality shines through the lines of *De Rerum Natura*. About all that Jerome has to say that might be reliable is that Cicero "amended" the work, which could mean that Cicero edited it, was responsible for its publication.

Further, it is impossible to know what in the philosophy of Lucretius is original. He is a spokesman for Epicurus (a philosopher of ancient Greece, of the 4th century B.C.; Epicurus is said to have produced a vast number of works, but only a very small fraction of them survive: Epicurus really comes to us by way of Lucretius, much as Plato is a spokesman for Socrates. And as with Plato and Socrates it is impossible to know how much of Lucretius is a "reproduction" of Epicurus, how much is Lucretius himself.

Yet, these reasons for Lucretius's obscurity don't really hold up to scrutiny. Almost nothing is known of Homer, yet Homer is one of the most popular poets the world has ever produced. And Plato endures — it hardly matters whether Socrates, as conveyed by Plato, is real or mainly imagined. Plato remains the most influential philosopher the Western world has ever produced.

There might be an even better reason for Lucretius's obscurity — his philosophy (whether it is entirely that of Epicurus or not) — the Epicurean philosophy — is one that entirely discounts religious belief as irrelevant. We know from earliest recorded history in the West that the ancient civilizations believed in deities, in a variety of gods and goddesses. Simultaneously, the ancient world of the Jews accepted a universe in which one God ruled. From the time of Constantine, Christianity was the official religion of the West, and so it remains to the present day. Meanwhile, all other countries of the world have a religious faith (Hinduism, Islam, Buddhism, etc.). Yet, Lucretius posits a Godless universe; he has always been the odd man out.

Indeed, the main message of his work is that he wishes to free man of his superstitions and of the fear of death. By "superstition" Lucretius means the notion that God (or, in his case, the Gods) created the world and continue in some way to direct what happens to that world and to our lives. Belief in God (the Gods) can be abolished, Lucretius says, by pointing out that natural

forces rule our world, that we and everything around us are simply comprised of
atoms that exist in empty space; our actions,
the actions of the world, have nothing to do
with the intervention of deities. As for fear
of death what, Lucretius argues, is to be
feared about annihilation; the nothingness
of death is neither good nor bad; we are not
there to experience it — just as we were not
there to experience all the time that occurred before our births. We should fear
only that which is tangible.

Why does he offer such a point of view in
verse? To make it more palatable.

Like the great religions and their beliefs,
the beliefs of Lucretius have endured as a
kind of eternal minority viewpoint. One
need only think of Karl Marx and his statement that "religion is the opiate of the
people," or listen to the arguments of a
modern atheist, or observe the actions of
modern men and women who live only for
the gratifications of this life, to realize the
justice of that statement. Yet, Lucretius differs from Marx in that he takes a very
jaundiced view of social strife and political
violence/struggle; Karl embraced them.
And Lucretius has been misunderstood:
"Epicureanism" has come to mean a life
devoted to pleasure rather than one devoted

to the contemplation of God. But, in proposing a life that rejects God, that sees life as an end in itself, Lucretius is not recommending hedonism as an alternative lifestyle. Lucretius's goal is the pursuit of intellectual pleasure (in fact, he takes a dim view of sexual pleasure or romantic love), which will in turn lead to a tranquility of mind, once superstition is banished. Lucretius, in his views, suggests the ways in which the universe may have been formed, the atomic structure of matter and the ways in which the various life forms would have emerged — in which views he predates modern science. In other words, he recommends not the pleasures of the flesh but the pleasures of the mind — and he was as good as his own recommendations. He offered speculations about the physical world that we now know to be true.

Every reader should sample Lucretius and *De Rerum Natura* to understand where this atheistic view of the universe comes from in the first place — then to realize that Lucretius is something more than a proponent of mindless sensual gratification, that he aims for much higher goals than those of many of the "godless" men who followed him. He offers the most perfect expression of the

Epicurean worldview in the literature of the West.

11
SAINT AUGUSTINE:
Confessions

WHO WAS SAINT AUGUSTINE?

Saint Augustine (354–430) — also known as Augustine of Hippo or by his Latin name Aurelius Augustinus — was one of the most important philosopher-theologians in the development of the early Christian church. His most notable writings are his autobiographical *Confessions* and *The City of God,* a Christian interpretation of history. Although he is a saint in the Roman Catholic church, his influence on Western theology has been so significant that both Roman Catholic and Protestant theologians consider him one of the founders of Western theology. His ideas have influenced the teachings of John, Calvin, Martin Luther and other Protestant reformers and his thinking is reflected in the work of such Western philosophers as Immanuel Kant and Blaise Pascal.

Augustine was born in the Roman provincial city of Tagaste (in what is now Algeria in North Africa) of a devout Catholic mother, Monica, and a pagan father, Patricius. Augustine studied Latin literature as a child and later traveled to Carthage to study rhetoric and philosophy. During his stay in Carthage, he became a teacher and established a relationship with a young woman with whom he had a son. He also lived a hedonistic lifestyle and embraced the Manichaean religion for a time. Manichaeism was a dualistic philosophy that advocated the principle of conflict between good and evil and a rational interpretation of Scripture. Its moral code was not strict.

Eventually, Augustine became disillusioned by his inability to reconcile contradictory Manichaeist beliefs, and he began to search for other theological doctrines. During this time he left Carthage for Rome and later Milan, where he met Ambrose, the distinguished Catholic bishop of Milan. Under the influence of Ambrose, Augustine turned to Christianity. In 391 he was ordained as a priest, and in 395 became bishop of Hippo Regius in northern Africa. He remained in Hippo as the leader of African Catholicism until his death in 430.

THE WORKS

Confessions

St. Augustine is one of the four great fathers of the Roman Catholic Church; the others are Ambrose, Jerome, and Gregory the Great. Mention these three others, however, and most non-Catholics would have difficulty identifying them; even most Catholics would have trouble remembering the details of their lives. But though he lived from the 4th to 5th centuries A.D., Augustine is still, 16 centuries later, one of the most famous men who ever lived. Even those who do not know his writings know the details of his life — for the reason that he has come to be regarded as the classic example of the man who struggles against the demands of the flesh only to emerge as the champion of the life of contemplation.

Augustine's education was in philosophy and rhetoric — the art of persuasion and public speaking. He then became a teacher of these subjects in both Tagaste and Carthage, but eventually he headed for Rome, where he believed the best rhetoricians were to be found. He quickly became disillusioned with Rome, and, through a stroke of good luck, became professor of rhetoric to the court of Milan. He was then just 30 years old. The academic chair of

Milan was one of prestige, one of the most notable in the Empire, and he probably could have moved on to a political career (as often happened to people in such high-profile academic posts).

Augustine continued his wayward, party-boy ways. Monica followed him to Milan, urged him to get married to a prominent woman of her choosing. He abandoned his mistress, then realized he would have to wait 2 years until his bride-to-be came of age — so took up with another woman. It is at this time that he uttered the famous prayer for which, across the centuries, he is best known: "Grant me chastity and continence, but not yet."

But it is not just the facts of this remarkable life that have engaged people throughout the centuries. Augustine is one of the most important figures in the development of Western Christianity — and not just for Roman Catholics. For Catholics, he is a saint and a "Doctor of the Church." Yet Protestants also revere his teachings on salvation and on grace.

Much of Augustine's writing survives, for example, we have many of his sermons; many of them of course involve religious controversies that have long since died away. But one of his works — *Confessions* —

retains an enduring popularity (as, for religious thinkers, does his *City of God*). In *Confessions* Augustine describes his wayward youth and his spiritual rebirth: it is the first and most influential religious autobiography that we know of, almost certainly the first "sinner saved" story, and it has delighted people for centuries. It has been a "standard" ever since Augustine wrote it, and many commentators have noted that, after *The Bible,* it is the most popular and enduring work of the Christian religion.

In both this work and in *City of God* — and this is their interest for us today — Augustine is a great synthesizer. His reading was immense, and he was greatly influenced by Platonism and Neoplatonism; he legitimized the philosophy of the Greeks as part of Christian intellectual thought and tradition. In describing his mother, he not only gives us a portrait of a kind of ideal Christian woman; as well, he suggests the role of women in the early church, a prominent role in a world we tend to think of as a patriarchy. He was, as well, instrumental in establishing the notion of original sin and its partner, the human will. He also commented on more worldly matters — for example, he is largely responsible for the notion that there can be a "just war" — to prevent wholesale destruction and slaughter. As well, he presented ideas that can be said to be as much philosophical as theological — that time exists only in the universe, in the creation of God, the world we see, that God alone exists in an eternal present.

Besides establishing certain doctrines that we now regard as inherent in Christianity (as if they were there from the beginning), Augustine offered views that now seem strikingly modern. He argued that, though the *Bible* was sacred, that it was the voice of God coming to us through the agency of man, it was not infallible — for the reason that its agency was human compositors who had written it centuries earlier. He argued: If something in the *Bible* contradicts what we know from science or from the exercise of our reason (a gift from God), then we must opt for the dictates of science and reason. For example: In considering the creation story in the *Bible,* Augustine says that he believes that everything was created simultaneously by God — not in 7 days. Augustine would have no trouble subscribing to the Big Bang theory.

Confessions should be read by everyone because it is a stimulating work from one of the greatest minds that ever lived. What he struggles against (the temptations of the flesh) are the struggles of every Christian, of everyone who tries to live, if not a religious life, at least a life of the mind — right against wrong, good against evil, the struggle to find truth in human life. But, in reading *Confessions,* readers should remember that much that we take for granted — in the Christian religion, in our view of the world, and in the best syntheses between religion and science — comes from this remarkable man.

12
MUHAMMAD:
The Koran

WHO WAS MUHAMMAD?

Muhammad (his name is sometimes spelled Mohammed; there are other variants) is the founder and greatest prophet of the Muslim religion, also called Islam, to which he has the same relation as Jesus does to Christianity. There are two important differences between the two men — although Muslims accord all conceivable earthly glory to Muhammad (his name in Arabic means "the praised one") and, though claims are made for his God-like nature, he is not in fact claimed to be divine or the son of Allah (the Muslim God); also, Muhammad was born about 600 years after Christ, and much more is known about the events of his life than we know about the events of the life of Jesus Christ.

He was born about 570 in Mecca and died in 632 in Medina. Both cities are in what we now call Saudi Arabia, and both are the holiest cities of Islam — all Muslims try to make a pilgrimage at least once in their lives to Mecca. Muhammad's family was fairly affluent, successful merchants and traders, and Muhammad, in his 20s and 30s, was a widely-traveled merchant himself. He married one of the clients, and together they had six children; after her death, he married other women and was not monogamous. But Muhammad was also monk-like in some of his habits: during the years that he was a merchant he often retreated to a cave near Mecca for quiet evenings of contemplation. In 610, when he was 40, Muslims believe, he was visited in the cave by the Angel Gabriel. Gabriel commanded him to listen to, then record, the words of Allah — rather as, in the Christian/Jewish tradition, God commands Moses to record the Ten Commandments. A crucial difference is that Moses received the Commandments in one solitary retreat; Muhammad continued the process of recording the words of Allah for 23 years after the first visitation from Gabriel, until the time of his own death.

The Koran

These words of God that Muhammad transcribed later became part of the *Qur'an* (or *Koran*), the Muslim bible (those parts of the *Qur'an* not written by Muhammad are the work of other Muslim prophets and scribes).

There is a great difference between Judaism and Christianity (the two great religions of the Western world) and Islam (the most prominent religion of the East. By 750, it had emerged as equal in world importance to the two other monotheistic religions). Judaism and Christianity, even though the latter borrows from the former as well as from pagan traditions, both claim to be the one true religion. Muhammad rejected neither of these religions — he regarded such people as Moses and Jesus as great prophets, accepted many of their essential teachings (in 620 he told his followers that he had been on a miraculous journey, had toured Heaven and Hell, and had spoken with earlier prophets such as Abraham. Muslims believe that he ascended to heaven for this experience from the mosque on Temple Mount in Jerusalem, hence the holiness of Jerusalem to Muslims as well as to Christians and Jews). But, despite his reverence for the Jewish prophets and for Jesus, Muhammad claimed that he had been sent by God to complete, perfect and refine their teachings. Put another way, Muhammad believed that he was a synthesizer, who was putting the "finishing touches" on what would become the world's one religion.

Islam was born in conditions of strife, rather than in the destruction of its leader. Muhammad, after his first vision of the Angel Gabriel, became (like Jesus) a preacher. Many of the religious and political leaders of Mecca persecuted him and his followers (the traditions of Islam claim that there were various attempts to assassinate Muhammad); they believed that they were trying to uphold an old and stable order of tribal rule and the sanctity of a multiplicity of gods. This persecution continued until the situation for Muhammad and his followers became so dangerous that in 622 he moved his community from Mecca to Medina (that journey is known to Muslims as the "Hijra"), where, with his followers, he formed the first Muslim community. For almost a decade this "state" was attacked by the forces of Mecca, bent on destroying it. Muhammad, with far fewer troops at his disposal, always prevailed in these battles (the battles themselves are regarded as holy in Muslim tradition), and in the end Muhammad and his followers took control of Medina. Other Arabian tribes (from different sectors of that country) began to send ambassadors to Medina, and gradually Arabia united under Muhammad's leadership. After Muhammad's death, Islam spread throughout what we now call the Middle East, and then to India, China and throughout the Far East. It is a curiosity of Western civilization that the Islamic world — the Muslim religion — has been ignored except when, at various stages in our history, it has intruded on our civilization. The events of 9/11 changed all that, and commentators who knew virtually nothing of Muhammad or Islam, commentators who had never read the *Qur'an,* made claims about Islam that are not true. For example, that it is a violent religion, that the teachings of Muhammad sanction terrorism. Simultaneously, and to the good, the events of 9/11 have stimulated readers to learn more about the Islamic world, about what the Muslim faith is all about.

Readers of the *Qur'an,* even those who only sample it, learn that, like Christianity, Islam is both an ethical and humane religion. Much of Muhammad's teachings will seem familiar to Christians or Jews — that

103

the laws of man are superseded by the laws of God, that we are all responsible to God for the conduct of our own lives, that love is the ideal by which we must try to interact with other people. Sometimes we must fight for our religion, but only to defend ourselves and that religion; we must never be attackers, never the ones who instigate strife and war. The *Qur'an* says: "Fight those who fight you."

The actions of someone like Osama bin Laden are thus, subtly, anti-Muslim. To conform to Muslim teachings, bin Laden claims to be defending Islam in a holy war — a *jihad* — against Western aggressors bent on destroying the Islamic world. Whether Muhammad would agree that the West had as its mission the destruction of Islam is an open question.

What is not in question is that Muhammad is one of the great prophets of history, who substituted a humane, monotheistic religion of love and respect for divine law for a pagan system of dog eat dog, and violence begetting violence. His message is as positive, for humans, as that of Jesus. And Christians are not unaccustomed, in the 2,000 years since his death, to corruptions of the teachings of Jesus, particularly the ways in which those words and teachings have been used to justify making war on others with whom the aggressor did not agree. Those of us who live in the world of Christians and Jews, a world in which an increasing number of Muslims are choosing to live, should have sampled the *Qur'an* — to be informed as to what Muhammad actually thought and said — and to understand that his God and his morality are not that different from our own.

13
The Arabian Nights

THE WORKS

The Arabian Nights

Like many works of antiquity or the Middle Ages, *The Arabian Nights* (also sometimes called *One Thousand and One Nights*) is a work by multiple authors, a compilation of stories, some of which are realistic, most of which are fantastic.

During the 8th century, Baghdad had become an important trading center for merchants from the Middle East, from Asia, Europe and Africa — and in turn it had become a very cosmopolitan place. During this time many different stories, originally folk stories, what we might today call fairy tales, from the various countries represented in Baghdad, were collected orally over a considerable period of time. A century later they were collected into a single book and translated into Arabic. Many people have been credited with that accomplishment;

the person most often mentioned is the famed storyteller Abu abd-Allah Muhammed el-Gahshigar. The framing story — of Queen Scheherazade — probably dates from the 14th century, and in this instance the author is unknown. But the authorship of *The Arabian Nights* has never been so interesting to the world as has the book itself.

The framing device of *The Arabian Nights* is perhaps its most famous story of all. During the Sassanid era a Persian king, Shahryar (who rules a country, an island, "between India and China"), is not necessarily an evil or malevolent person: he is made so by events. He discovers that his wife and her lover are plotting to kill him — his wife is not just faithless, she is also guilty of treason; he has her and her lover executed, and thereafter believes in the universal faithlessness and treachery of women. Shahryar instructs his grand vizier (his most trusted adviser and the greatest administrative official in his kingdom) to find him a new wife every day. After spending the night with the wife, he has her executed. This practice continues for some time (the story never says how long), until the vizier's beautiful but also ingenious daughter Scheherazade devises a scheme to outwit the king and, in doing so, stop the killings. She herself offers to become Shahryar's next wife, and is accepted. Every night, in their marriage chambers, Scheherazade tells Shahryar stories, but she is careful to stop at dawn before ending the story — and she stops with a cliffhanger — the king spares her life, so that, the following night, he may hear the rest of the story. Having finished one story halfway through the evening, she starts another — until, years hence, she has given birth to three of their sons. Convinced of the faithfulness of Scheherazade (a woman he loves, as she loves him), he revokes his decree, at her request pardons her. From malevolence, and through his wife's inspired trickery, he comes to find love. All's well that ends well.

But if this is the most famous story of *The Arabian Nights,* there are others — such as "Ali Baba and the Forty Thieves" or "Sinbad the Sailor" — that are almost as famous. Most of *The Arabian Nights* is a hodge-podge — of love stories and comedies and tragedies and historic legends; also included are even some famous religious (Muslim) myths. Some of the stories involve magic and the supernatural; yet within legendary places and fables there are accounts of those we know to have been real people. But, as there were multiple authors with multiple agendas, there cannot be said to be a discernible theme.

The stories were first brought to the West in the early 18th century when they were published in a French translation. The first substantial version in English was published in the late 19th century. It has become one of the world's most popular literary works.

What is its significance? If by a significant book we mean one that changed the world, changed the way at least some people think and feel, then it must be said that *The Arabian Nights* has virtually no significance whatsoever. But to say so is to lose sight of a more subtle distinction. The stories have inspired countless movies and TV specials; they have even inspired some composers of music. Movies based on *The Arabian Nights* will be released in 2006 and 2007. The gifted playwright and director Mary Zimmerman has presented her own staged version of many of the stories, and her play has been popular throughout the country.

Perhaps the more interesting question to ask is why *The Arabian Nights* endures and why it continues to inspire those who make our movies and television programs, compose our music, and write our plays.

For some reason, most people like stories

of the exotic, the legendary, the supernatural. But there have been many such stories in the history of the world, and only a handful endure (the stories of Homer would be a good example). Something about the stories of *The Arabian Nights* attracts people to them. The psychologist Jung might have said that they touch on our collective memories as humans, the myths about human behavior that, over the centuries, we have come to accept.

Whatever the reason, *The Arabian Nights,* written centuries ago in lands most of us do not know, continue to intrigue and delight modern readers — and reading them can provoke the reader to ask the same kind of questions: what here touches on what is universal in all of our experience?

14
MURASAKI SHIKIBU:
The Tale of Genji

WHO WAS MURASAKI SHIKIBU?

It should be very unlikely that Murasaki Shikibu — she is sometimes called Lady Murasaki by her modern admirers — would be remembered by the world today. She lived in the 10th and 11th centuries (around 974 to around 1014 or 1025) in the imperial court of Japan during what is now called the Heian Period. Her father was an official of that court, and she was, therefore, a Japanese aristocrat. Because her mother had died young (it was the custom of the time for children to be raised by their mother; married couples lived separately), Murasaki was raised by her father. It was obvious to her father that she was very intelligent; so he gave her an education considered at the time more appropriate for a man than for a woman. She, too, when she was no longer a child, was also a servant of the court: she served as a lady-in-waiting to the Empress.

What saves Murasaki from obscurity — from disappearing into the mists of history — is that she was also a notable novelist and poet. Although much of her verse still exists ("The Murasaki Shikibu Collection," published after her death, is a collection of 128 of her poems), it is her novel, *The Tale of Genji,* that has brought her immortality. Everyone acknowledges that it is the first novel of which we know that was written by a woman. Some critics go further, discounting the claims of Homer and other Greeks and Romans, as well as those who wrote prose narratives during the early Middle Ages, and say that *The Tale of Genji* is very likely the first modern novel. It is, the first book that is recognizably what modern readers would call a novel. Quite an accomplishment for an obscure female servant of the Japanese court who lived three centuries before Chaucer!

THE WORKS

The Tale of Genji

The tradition is that the Lady Murasaki wrote *The Tale of Genji,* and her poems, for other ladies of the aristocracy — to amuse them, to give them a diversion in what was otherwise a rather sedentary life. Then, as now, women were thought to like love stories, and the novel is the story of the aristocratic Genji, his life and (most of all) his loves. Some literary commentators have noted that *The Tale of Genji* has no plot, that the story covers Genji and his life, as well it tells us what happens to his descendants after his death, but the events unfold not so much through a series of plot devices (there are no cliff-hangers in *Genji*) but rather as a sequence of events that happen because the characters are growing older, moving through life. But to a contemporary reader, this method seems very modernist — the great novel of Proust, *Remembrance of Things Past,* and those of the novelists he influenced, are not very different. We follow characters as they live their lives; they don't really move from one plot contrivance to the next. That is the method of second-rate modern fiction — not the greatest works of our greatest novelists.

Despite the fact that she was writing in a kind of void (as far as we know, there were no predecessor novels to guide her), Murasaki maintains remarkable consistency. Even though there are more than 400 characters in her novel, she focuses on Genji, on her subsidiary major characters, and they are recognizably the same people throughout the novel. Even though, as was traditional in polite society of the time, characters are rarely named, are known only by their professions, their position in society.

Genji is a son of the Japanese emperor, and the *Tale of Genji* is the story of how he ascends to the greatest honor in the land. He never becomes the emperor himself, but the emperor knows that he is the illegitimate son of Genji and the great love of his life, Lady Fujitsubo — Genji's stepmother who secretly becomes his mistress — a woman he continues to love throughout his life, despite his adventures with other women. His son, the emperor, at what might be called the dramatic conclusion of the novel, raises Genji's rank to the highest possible in the court of Japan.

The Tale of Genji is still regarded by the Japanese as the greatest novel of their culture, and, though Murasaki's language is difficult (Heian Japanese is exalted, classical and grammatically complex), therefore difficult to translate into other languages, the novel does exist in notable English and other language translations. In its translations into various languages, both Eastern and Western, it continues to fascinate the world. Not just for its interesting story — which is epic-like in its breadth. It fascinates us, too, for its glimpse into a feudal world that most of us can barely comprehend; the potency of that long-ago world is increased, not diminished, by its being set in the Japanese Imperial Court, by its concentration on the ruling class of its time. This world is as "foreign" as anything could be to the modern reader. And yet, the novel grips us — we care what happens to Genji and to his compatriots.

The secret of *The Tale of Genji*'s continued hold on modern readers is almost certainly traceable to Lady Murasaki's genius in conveying the psychological truth of her characters and of their actions. Her story is compelling because we recognize personality traits in her characters not that different from our own — even though they are men and women of the 11th century, living in a world most of us can't even begin to imagine. They seem to be like us, and, in saying that, we recognize that we are in the hands of a master. The novel, first and foremost, is the art form in which we examine not so much the adventures of human beings, or the events, real or imagined, of their lives — as it is the form in which the greatest novelists show us man's reactions, what he learns or fails to learn from those life adventures and events. The novel, we might say, is the form in which we trace the ways in which man develops his consciousness of the world and of himself.

In this kind of artistic effort, Lady Murasaki may be said to be our first novelist of the consciousness and, by any measure, one of the greatest. Any reader should have sampled her work to understand what other definers of the human soul have had as their example of the supreme mastery of their craft.

15

TUROLD:
The Song of Roland

THE WORKS

The Song of Roland

The Song of Roland (in French: *La Chanson de Roland* — song/chanson in the sense of ballad; it is likely that, originally, it was composed to be sung) is a French epic poem (it dates from about 1050) that was probably written by someone called Turold. His name is mentioned in the last line of the poem, though it could well be that Turold is simply the person who brought together a host of variants on the Roland story. It is the first great work of French literature and is universally regarded as the greatest "chanson de geste," one of a series of epic poems that helped to create the legend of Charlemagne during the period that we now call the Late Middle Ages.

These works commemorate Charlemagne's life many centuries after that life, and the various poems, though largely fictional, do contain a basic core of historic truth. In this way, they are like the British stories of King Arthur — except that Arthur lived earlier than Charlemagne, and the most famous work about Arthur was written 3 centuries after Turold compiled *The Song of Roland.*

There is one other, even more crucial, difference. Scholars are divided about whether or not King Arthur actually lived — or whether he was a war lord who was elevated, in myth, to kingly stature — or whether he is a composite who, in legend, became one person, a necessary hero to the British nation, which required some sense of itself as a distinct people with a glorious past.

Charlemagne may serve the same function for the French and Germans, the peoples of Central Europe, but no such controversy exists about whether or not Charlemagne actually existed. He did exist. He lived from 742 to 814. He was King of the Franks from 768 until his death, King of the Lombards from 774 until his death, and in 800 he was appointed (by Pope Leo) the first Holy Roman Emperor. Charlemagne, assisted by his grandfather and father before him, conquered most of Western Europe; his family established the first great and stable kingdom after the Fall of the Western Roman Empire. Charlemagne is an authentic hero, the greatest figure of what we sometimes call the Dark Ages and at other times call the Early Middle Ages. Because he was so notable an historic figure, legends about him continued to develop centuries after his death.

The Song of Roland tells an interesting story. Much as *The Iliad* deals with an historic (though perhaps mythical) battle in Greek history, so *The Song of Roland* deals with a battle in French history — the Battle of Roncesvalles (Roncevaux) in 778, which was really an insignificant encounter between the French and the Basques — Turold makes it an earth-shattering event. Charlemagne and his army have been fighting in Spain for 7 years; they have conquered all of Spain except for Saragossa. Roland, one of the 12 senior knights of the court, and Charlemagne's nephew, proposes that Charlemagne send his stepfather, Ganelon, to negotiate peace terms. Incensed that Roland has proposed him for what is actually a very dangerous task (previous ambassadors have been murdered by the Saracens) Ganelon plots his stepson's destruction. As Charlemagne's army crosses the Pyrenees, the rear guard of that army (which includes Roland and his fellow senior knights) is surrounded by a huge and overwhelming Saracen force. Roland is the commander of this rear guard, and he fights nobly and heroically, even as he is certain to be defeated. His motivation is that he lives according to a code of honor, that he cannot admit defeat even in the face of overwhelming odds — and he can revel in the glory of his future renown — and in doing so he refuses the advice of his best friend Oliver (another of the 12 senior knights) to call Charlemagne to his aid. As a result of Ganelon's conniving, the rear guard is essentially decimated, and Roland and his comrades die. Charlemagne avenges his men. When he returns to France, he breaks the news to Roland's fiancée, Aude, Oliver's sister, and she dies of grief and shock. *The Song of Roland* ends with the execution of Ganelon for his treason.

A rollicking good story to be sure, and it is told in a clear and direct style that engages the reader. Besides well-rendered scenes of conflict, it involves compelling stories of betrayal (Ganelon and Roland) and stories of friendship (Roland and Oliver) and of love (Roland and Aude). But these are not the only reasons to read *The Song of Roland*. More than any other work from the continent of Europe during the

Middle Ages, it gives us the basic tenets of chivalry that was to flower in the centuries after its composition. The world, we are shown, is corrupt; there is selfishness everywhere; betrayal of one human being by another is commonplace — yet there are those who, like Charlemagne and his knights, behave with honor and honesty, who attempt to love and serve the good, who strive for a perfection of behavior — who try to be true servants of Christ. As being such a servant often involves battles and bloodshed, and as the men (and their women) are knights and servants of God's appointed master on earth, the king. Some modern readers will have difficulty reconciling the kind of morality involved with their own lives. One must accept the battles and bloodshed as givens of the time — just as they are givens of the time in which we live.

Readers coming to *The Song of Roland* for the first time are likely to be entranced by its story — just as all of us are captivated by the legends of Arthur. But within the grandeur and nobility of the story, there is a kind of longing, and striving, to live life well. *The Song of Roland* was enormously popular from the time of its writing until the 14th century — a space of 200 years; and, since then, it has endured. Readers should remember that this book, *The da Vinci Code* of its day, is most of all interesting for the ways in which it shows different men learning the appropriate ways for a man to live — it implicitly asks: What are appropriate actions and attitudes and beliefs? As so many of these questions survive to the present day, it is instructive for any reader to learn the ways in which they were asked nearly a millennium ago and what the world of chivalry actually involved.

16
St. Thomas Aquinas:
Summa Theologica

WHO WAS ST. THOMAS AQUINAS?

St. Thomas Aquinas (1225–1274) was a prominent churchman of the 13th century, and he lived the typical life of such a figure — except in some very important respects: his parents were Italian aristocrats, and his uncle was abbot of the Benedictine monastery at Monte Cassino; he had very auspicious beginnings. The only conflict of his early life was that while studying at the University of Naples, he was drawn to, then completely attracted to, the new order of the Dominicans, and engaged in a rather serious fight with his family about his decision to become a Dominican monk (he was held captive in one of his family's castles — to make him see reason; it was his family's expectation that he would one day succeed his uncle as abbot at Monte Cassino).

Once Aquinas had begun life as a Dominican, when he was 17, he went on to an illustrious career. His superiors realized that he showed unusual promise as a theologian, and they sent him to Cologne to study with Albertus Magnus, the great theologian/philosopher of the time. For several years he stayed with Albertus, both as student and then as acolyte. Aquinas was designated a Doctor of Theology in 1256, and from then until his death in 1274 he never stopped working. He traveled throughout Western Europe teaching and lecturing; he also traveled constantly on the business of his Order, to which he became increasingly valuable. Despite all of this activity, Aquinas still found time to write, and, given his learning and his reputation, he was often consulted about affairs of state and matters of theology by the reigning powers of the Church, including the Pope himself.

THE WORKS

Summa Theologica

During his lifetime St. Thomas Aquinas was considered a great philosopher as well as a great theologian. He worked on his best-known work, *Summa Theologica,* during the period 1266–1273, leaving it unfinished at the time of his death. He claimed to have had a mystical vision in late 1273. He said of it, "I cannot go on . . . . All that I have written seems to me like so much straw compared to what I have seen and what has been revealed to me." Despite his learning and accomplishments, Aquinas remained a model of Christian humility.

If anything his fame became even greater after his death. His fellow theologians elevated him to a position within the historic Church comparable to that of Paul and Augustine; he was canonized in 1323. At the Council of Trent (1545–63), *Summa Theologica* was put on the altar next to the *Bible;* in 1567, Pope Pius V compared him in importance to the four great Latin fathers of the Church; and in 1880, Aquinas was declared patron of all Roman Catholic educational institutions. No one doubts his renown as a theologian; some people might even say that he is the greatest theologian the Roman Catholic Church has ever produced.

But, Aquinas lived in the 13th century — even Roman Catholics might ask what relevance he has to us today. And, Protestants are even more likely to ask such a question.

Perhaps too much is made in our time of the differences between Catholics and Protestants. At the time that Aquinas lived there was only one Church, the one that he served so brilliantly. And the "protest" of Martin Luther (who lived almost 3 centuries later) had much to do with what Luther saw as the corruption of the Church. More important for us, Luther regarded certain Catholic beliefs, particularly those involved in various of the sacraments, as too mystical. Luther believed that the individual must come to some truths on his own, not always follow the dictates of a priesthood he did not believe had been ordained by God. But the core beliefs themselves were not challenged — the essentials of Christianity are the same in either church. For example, in the mass, during communion, Catholics believe that their priest achieves mystical union with Christ; Protestants believe only that they are remembering Christ at the Last Supper. But both kinds of Christian churches regard that sacrament, whatever actually happens in its practice, as crucial to their faith. Aquinas's skill, in defining the core tenets of Christianity, is relevant to any kind of Christian.

Aquinas did not write the *Summa* for his fellow theologians and philosophers. He set out to write a manual — what we would today call a textbook — of the main theological teachings of his time; he attempted to give the reasons for all components of the Christian faith. Because, by any measure, he was a genius, he did not just offer the accepted wisdom but refined and reworked it to such a degree that his explanations exist as if for the first time. It can truly be said that he sums up Christianity — and does it so brilliantly that his words resonate with us even at the present time. The *Summa* is in three parts: 1) The Nature of God and the Universe That He Created; 2) Human Activity and Ethics; and 3) Christ and the Sacraments.

In presenting his explanations and definitions, Aquinas also attempts to encompass the philosophy of the Greeks. He lived at a time when the scholarly world was beginning to discover such philosophers from the past as Aristotle. Aquinas believed that knowledge of God was through revelation — God's revealing of Himself to an individual when that individual is in a state of grace — that is, has practiced right behavior pleasing to God. But, bringing in Aristotle, he believed that grace (the moving by man toward God) can happen as a result of an examination of God's created order. The Christian says: Certain aspects of God can be revealed to us only by the *Bible.* The Aristotelian says: The "condition" of God's creation is revealed to us only by study of that creation. Aquinas attempts to reconcile these two views, and, in this, he is the great synthesizer — and his synthesis survives to the present day.

Anyone, whether Christian or not, who wishes to understand Christianity — one of the world's great religions, perhaps its most influential religion — must read the *Summa,* to understand the remarkable description of Christianity, an amalgam of the classical and medieval world views, that Aquinas created.

17
MARCO POLO:
The Adventures of Marco Polo

WHO WAS MARCO POLO?

Marco Polo (1254–1324) was a Venetian trader and explorer who was one of the first Westerners to travel the Silk Road to China or, as he called it, Cathay. He wrote a book, *The Travels of Marco Polo* (*Il Milione*) describing his travels, which offered Europeans some of their earliest information about Cathay.

Born in Venice into a family of merchants and traders, Marco Polo accompanied his father, Nicolò, and his uncle, Maffeo, on their second trading mission to eastern Asia. Earlier, before Marco's birth, the two brothers had traveled to Asia where they had met the Mongol ruler, Kublai Khan, in China. The Khan invited them to return; they prepared for another expedition that included Marco, then 17 years old. The trio set out across the deserts and mountains of Asia, and after more than three years they

129

reached Kublai Khan's summer palace in Shangdu.

For almost 20 years the Polos, Marco in particular, served the Khan as diplomats and aides. Eventually, they started worrying about returning home safely — the Khan was aging, and if he died, the Polos were afraid that his enemies might capture them. The Khan finally agreed to their leaving in 1292, provided they escorted a Chinese princess who was to marry a Persian king.

Their return trip began on a ship from China to Singapore; they went north of Sumatra, around the southern tip of India, and across the Arabian Sea and the Gulf of Oman. The Polos left the wedding party and traveled overland to a port on the Black Sea from which they sailed to Istanbul and then traveled on to Venice. The Polos had been away from home for 24 years.

Upon their arrival home in 1295, Marco joined the Venetian Army in its fight against Genoa. In 1298 he was captured and imprisoned in Genoa. During his 2 years in custody, Marco dictated his accounts of his travels to a fellow inmate, Rustichello of Pisa, who translated the book into Old French, the literary language of the time in Italy, and entitled it *Le divisament du monde* (*The Description of the World*). Later the book was translated into other languages, including an English edition, *The Travels of Marco Polo;* it was distributed throughout Europe. The book enjoyed instant popularity.

After he was released from prison in 1299, Marco returned to Venice to a large home in the central quarter, which he shared with his father and uncles. He became a wealthy merchant who financed other expeditions, but he personally never again left Venice. He married a woman from a respected noble family, and the couple had three children, all of whom later married into noble families. It is believed that he wrote a new version of his book in Italian between 1310 and 1320, which was translated into Latin by a Franciscan friar before being lost. The Latin edition was then translated back into Italian.

In January of 1324, Marco Polo died and was buried in the Church of San Lorenzo.

THE WORKS

The Travels of Marco Polo

Marco Polo's account of his travels to Cathay and throughout Asia is divided into four books: Book One describes the Middle Eastern and Central Asian lands through which the Polos traveled on their way to China; Book Two depicts China and the court of Kublai Khan; Book Three provides secondhand accounts of some of the Far Eastern coastal regions, including Japan, India, Sri Lanka, Southeast Asia, and the east coast of Africa; and Book Four recounts wars among the Mongols and describes some of the far northern regions such as Russia. Each book, in addition to being a geography of the region, describes the politics, agriculture, economy, military capability, burial system, religious beliefs, and cultural practices of the region.

Marco was receptive to new ideas and marveled at some of the Asian practices that had never been seen in Europe. He described the Kublai Khan's prosperous and advanced empire. He discussed the Khan's postal system of courier stations and horseback riders across the kingdom, relaying messages from one station to another. He commented on many Chinese and Asian customs, including the mining and use of coal as fuel (Marco called coal "black stones"), Chinese paper money bearing the seal of the emperor, credit systems, iron manufacturing, salt production, papermaking, printing, and a canal-based internal transportation system. At that point in history, China had greater wealth and a much more complex social structure than any country or region in Europe.

Because many of Marco Polo's stories of what he discovered in Asia seemed so far-fetched to many of his readers, many Europeans doubted his veracity. Some even questioned whether he had even traveled to China. Many thought that he probably gathered information from Arabs who were Silk Road travelers. There was a flourishing trade between the Middle East and the Far East, and merchants and travelers were known to enjoy relating stories of their adventures in great detail. Although Marco's reference to Japan by its Chinese name, "Zipang" or "Cipangu," is considered to be the first mention of Japan in Western literature, many scholars thought that Marco could have learned about Japan from fellow merchants on the trade routes. In the 18th and 19th centuries, however, travelers to Asia confirmed what he had written.

Regardless of such questions about its authenticity, *The Travels of Marco Polo* had an enormous impact when it was first published. Even though the Polos were not the first Europeans to reach China, Marco's book was acknowledged to be the most important account of the world beyond

Europe at the time. Marco's skill in conveying new or unknown cultures, plus his willingness to travel through uncharted areas in unknown weather to unfamiliar lands, gave his travelogue credence and appeal to most European readers. Today, the book has become a useful account of the history, geography, politics, and social customs of 13th century China.

Marco Polo introduced Europe to paper currency, coal as fuel, a courier postal system, papermaking, printing, and the compass. On a more domestic level, legend has it that Marco introduced new Chinese products to Italy, namely, ice cream and spaghetti and other pastas.

The Travels of Marco Polo also exerted tremendous influence on geographic exploration by suggesting new possibilities for Western explorers. Geographers incorporated some of Marco's information into maps during the later Middle Ages, notably the Catalan World Map of 1375, and his book and the resulting maps were later read by Henry the Navigator and other cartographers. This contribution to more accurate maps was only part of his legacy, however; Marco's system of measuring distances by day's journey was, in fact, quite accurate and became the regular practice of later explorers.

The book and its tales of wealth and adventures also captured the imagination of explorers. Marco's description of the Far East and its riches inspired Christopher Columbus two centuries later to seek a western route to those lands. Christopher Columbus owned a copy of *The Travels* to which he added numerous annotations. Even today *The Travels of Marco Polo* is one of the most complete records of geographic exploration in Asia and the Far East, and many geographers and topographers call Marco Polo's work the precursor of scientific geography.

Marco Polo himself may have best described his achievement when he said in his own book, "I believe . . . that we should come back, so that men might know the things that are in the world, since, as we have said in the first chapter of the book, no other man, Christian or Saracen, Mongol or pagan, has explored so much of the world as Messer Marco, son of Messer Niccolo Polo, great and noble citizen of the city of Venice."

18
DANTE:
The Divine Comedy

WHO WAS DANTE?

Dante (1265–1321), whose full name was Dante Alighieri, was born into an aristocratic family in Florence, Italy. At age 12 Dante was promised in marriage to Gemma Di Manetto Donati, a common practice at that time — he did eventually marry her, and they had four children. At age 9, however, Dante had met 8 year-old Beatrice Portinari; she became the central figure in an unrequited love affair from afar — she was, as well, the inspiration of his poetry.

Although little is known about his education, Dante later revealed a knowledge of music, painting, Tuscan poetry, Provencal minstrels, and of Latin culture, particularly the work of Virgil. In 1295 he became a member of the Guild of Apothecaries as a doctor and pharmacist, because Florentine law required that a noble wishing to enter politics and assume public office had to

belong to the *Corporazioni de Arti e Mestieri.*
Dante never had any intention of pursuing
those professions, but his membership
served its purpose: for several years he held
various important public offices and participated in the civic and cultural life of Florence.

During this time Florence was undergo-
ing political turmoil because two factions
were competing for control of the city.
Dante allied himself with the Guelfs, the
faction that endorsed Florentine political
autonomy and supported the papacy. The
opposition, the Ghibellines, were backed by
the Holy Roman Emperor. After defeating
the Ghibellines, the Guelfs, driven by
economic and family interests, split into two
groups: the White Guelfs, the group to
which Dante belonged, and the Black
Guelfs. By the end of the 13th century the
Pope was backing the Black Guelfs, who
were in turn more strongly committed to
the Pope than were the moderate White
Guelfs. The White Guelfs were forced into
exile, and for the next 20 years Dante lived
in various Italian cities but never returned
to Florence, the city to which he had devoted a great deal of public service. In 1319
he moved to Ravenna where he completed
The Divine Comedy before his death in 1321.

THE WORKS

The Divine Comedy

Although Dante was a prolific writer, *The Divine Comedy* (*La divina commedia*) is considered his greatest work and has been called the primary epic of Italian literature. Dante's epic (a long narrative poem told in dignified and exalted style) is composed of three books — *Inferno* (Hell), *Purgatorio* (Purgatory), and *Paradiso* (Paradise) — of 33 cantos each with a single introductory canto for a total of more than 14,000 lines. The cantos have an internal rhythm because of their three-line *terza rima* stanzas, a verse form Dante developed. In this verse form the first and third lines of each stanza rhyme with the middle line of the preceding stanza.

The Divine Comedy is a first-person account of the poet's travels through the three realms of the dead; it all takes place during Holy Week in the Spring of 1300. The Roman poet Virgil is Dante's guide through Hell and Purgatory, and Beatrice, Dante's ideal woman and symbol of pure love, is his guide through Paradise. The epic begins with Dante's finding himself lost in a dark forest, a symbol of what he thought was his own unworthy life and the evil of society. On Good Friday Dante meets Virgil, who promises to lead him through the Underworld.

Dante begins this journey by passing through the Gate of Hell and crossing the river Acheron into Hell itself. Virgil then steers Dante through the nine concentric circles of Hell, each one representing a progressively greater evil and each one punished appropriately. Each circle is populated by crowds of individuals, some of whom are from the past but most of whom are from Dante's time, who are being punished for their sins. The journey culminates in the center of the earth at the seat of Satan.

The poets escape the Inferno by riding Lucifer though the center of the earth into the southern hemisphere on Easter Sunday. Virgil now guides Dante through the seven terraces of Purgatory, which purges each of the representative sins. The seven terraces correspond to the seven deadly sins: pride, envy, wrath, sloth, avarice, gluttony, and lust. At the top of the terraces is the Garden of Eden where, because he is a pagan, Virgil is denied access and where Beatrice becomes Dante's guide. Beatrice leads Dante through the concentric spheres of Heaven. Beatrice leaves Dante at one of the levels after which he ascends beyond physical existence to a plane of existence where he meets God and receives an understanding of divine and of human nature.

Although in some sense *The Divine Comedy* is a love poem extolling Beatrice's innocent beauty and her moral power to lead Dante to supreme goodness, it is also a personal account of Dante's spiritual development and of the preoccupation of the 13th and 14th century Christianity with life after death. Dante's goal was to create a poem that reflected the world of the Christian God of his time. Part of his philosophical approach was influenced by his belief in the reconciliation between Aristotelian thought and Christian faith espoused by St. Thomas Aquinas.

For many scholars, *The Divine Comedy* is significant in that it is thought to be the last great work of literature in the Middle Ages — indeed, it is often cited as a summary of medieval thought — as well as the first great work of the Renaissance. Scholars have lauded the work not only for its innovative and magnificent poetry but also for its immense learning.

Dante wrote *The Comedy* in his regional Tuscany dialect — he was making a statement, that the Italian language was rich enough to convey the highest form of expression and thought. Because of his choice, the Tuscan dialect became the standard for the Italian language, especially in the arts. His choice of language also partly explains the word "comedy" in the title. In Dante's times, scholarly works were written in Latin; works in any other language were presumed to be comedic in content. As well, the word "comedy" was used to describe writings that portrayed an ordered universe in which events ended in ultimate good. The adjective "divine" was added to the original title on the publication of a beautiful edition of Dante's epic in 1555.

As an important thinker and writer, Dante exerted a great deal of influence on later writers: Geoffrey Chaucer and John Milton imitated Dante's works. Interest in *The Divine Comedy* and Dante's other writings languished during the Enlightenment of the 18th century. The Enlightenment was a historical intellectual movement that advocated rationality as the basis of aesthetics, ethics, and logic. The intellectual leaders of this movement proposed to lead the world out of the period of irrationality, tradition, and superstition that they called the Dark Ages and into a world of progress. Dante seemed irrelevant.

The romantic writers of the 19th century rediscovered Dante. Dante and his work influenced the thinking and work of many 19th century writers, including William Blake, Longfellow, Byron, Shelley, Tennyson, Victor Hugo, and Friedrich Schlegel, the German poet and critic. Dante also influenced such 20th century writers as T. S. Eliot, Ezra Pound, Samuel Beckett, and James Joyce. Modern poets, including Seamus Heaney, Robert Pinsky, and William Merwin, have used translations of Dante in their work.

The Divine Comedy and other writings by Dante have survived for more than 6 centuries. Dante's influence on subsequent writers and philosophies has been so great that his work, particularly *The Divine Comedy,* affects Western Christian thinking about the afterlife even today.

19
PETRARCH:
Canzoniere

WHO WAS PETRARCH?

Francesco Petrarch (1304–1374) was an Italian scholar, poet, and humanist; he was, as well, a major cause of the flowering of what we now call the Renaissance. As a scholar, Petrarch rediscovered and emphasized the greatness of classical literature: he was responsible for the first Latin translation of Homer, and he found some undiscovered manuscripts of the Latin writers Cicero and Livy. His interest in classical literature inspired him to collect these and other ancient manuscripts that had been forgotten in monastic and cathedral libraries and to build a private library that became the model for such famous libraries as the Laurentian in Florence, St. Mark's in Venice, and that of the Vatican in Rome.

He displayed his displeasure about the neglect of ancient manuscripts when he said: "Each famous author of antiquity whom I recover places a new offense and another cause of dishonor to the charge of earlier generations, who, not satisfied with their own disgraceful barrenness, permitted the fruit of other minds, and the writings that their ancestors had produced by their toil and application, to perish through insufferable neglect. Although they had nothing of their own to hand down to those who were to come after, they robbed posterity of its ancestral heritage."

Born in Arezzo, Italy, Petrarch spent his early years in a village near Florence, because his father, Petracco, a clerk of one of the courts of justice in Florence, had been expelled from Florence by the conquering Black Guelph political faction, the same group that had exiled Dante during the same period. After a short time in Arezzo, Petracco took the family to Pisa, then to Avignon, France. At his father's insistence, Petrarch studied law at Montpellier and Bologna, but his interests were really focused on writing and on Latin literature. This interest so infuriated his father that he burned a number of his son's favorite ancient manuscripts. When his father died, Petrarch abandoned his law studies and turned to writing and his real scholarly interests.

Petrarch returned to Avignon and took minor offices in the Church. He thus received a small income from the Church while enjoying the social life of Avignon. It was during this time that he encountered Laura for the first time. In 1327 in the church of Sainte-Claire d'Avignon, Petrarch saw a woman named Laura with whom he fell in love — at a distance. Although it is not known whether Laura actually existed as a person, many scholars have speculated that she may have been Laura de Noves, the wife of Hugues de Sade. Petrarch's realistic portrait of Laura in his poems expresses his joy in her presence but also his pain in their unrequited relationship. In his "Letter to Posterity," Petrarch wrote, "I struggled constantly with an overwhelming but pure love affair . . ."

In the early 1330s Petrarch began to travel throughout France and Germany, recording his observations in letters to friends. In 1336 he traveled to Rome for the first time; he settled there, and during this period in his life he became well-known as a scholar and poet. In 1341 he was crowned the first poet laureate of modern times, an honor that required his traveling as a kind of diplomat. His position and fame enabled him to introduce western Europe to classical antiquity, which he saw as a cultural framework for the study of human thought and action.

Petrarch was a devout Christian — he took minor orders, and he served the Church in various positions; he saw no conflict between realizing human potential and practicing religious faith. His reconciliation of his two "faiths" was the beginning of humanism and an integral part of Renaissance thought. He traveled to courts in Italy, France, Germany, and Spain, helping to spread the Renaissance point of view, while collecting Latin manuscripts and popularizing classical literary works that had languished, unknown, for centuries.

THE WORKS

Canzoniere

Petrarch wrote most of his works in Latin, but Latin did not allow him to express his personal thoughts and observations. More important are his works in Italian, particularly his love lyrics to the mysterious Laura, which are collected in the *Canzoniere* (*Book of Songs*).

The *Canzoniere* is a chronological account of Petrarch's passion for Laura. The tone alternates between physical pleasure and religious feeling, mirroring the individual's uneasiness when faced with both spiritual love and physical desire. There are 366 poems, including sonnets, odes, songs, madrigals, and ballads, divided into two parts: The first part includes 263 poems written during Laura's lifetime and offers a chronological account of the poet's continuing passion for her. The second part consists of poems written after Laura's death — it portrays Laura as a guide, leading her lover toward God and salvation. Throughout the work there is a sense of juxtaposition of spiritual love and human physical pleasure.

Canzoniere is often regarded as the first work to portray modern man emerging from a medieval world into the Renaissance period, because it shows human uncertainties, frailties, and indomitable spirit.

The *Canzoniere* is one of Europe's most influential works. Petrarch perfected the verse forms of the sonnet and the ode, and he expressed the joy and pain of human love in a sequence of related poems. Many subsequent European poets and writers drew on Petrarch's legacy of the courtly representation of spiritual yet human love for an exalted and unattainable woman. The work of Chaucer, Shakespeare, Pope, Byron, and Rossetti reflect Petrarch's influence.

These poets, as well as Renaissance poets Thomas Wyatt and Edmund Spenser and the Romantic poet Lord Byron, demonstrate in their work the extended metaphors introduced by Petrarch. Spenser and Wyatt were early translators of Petrarch's sonnets and songs.

One of Petrarch's primary contributions to literature was his use and refinement of Italian in his verse — despite the fact that he knew Latin well and did much of his writing in Latin, particularly his scholarly treatises and letters. He understood that the use of Italian would permit more personal expression of his feelings and infuse his love poetry with an immediacy and significance that he could not achieve with Latin. The Italian language allowed him to portray Laura as a real woman, not just a spiritual symbol, and to define true emotions rather than medieval conventions.

Petrarch was also a noted scholar. His interest in classical writings led him to realize that Platonic thought and Greek studies provided a cultural framework for his own thinking; he believed it could help other men as well. He became a student and commentator on ancient Greek and Roman works that emphasized the pre-Christian concept of man as the central focus of life.

These studies were instrumental in his becoming an active participant in the development of Christian humanism as an outcome of the Italian Renaissance. Often called the father of humanism, Petrarch believed that the human individual could lead a life of self-reliance and meaning. He did not minimize nor ignore Christian belief, but neither did he see a contradiction between faith and human individualism. His defining and espousing humanism during the flowering of the Italian Renaissance was the beginning of a movement that had a profound effect on the Renaissance, the Reformation, the Enlightenment, and on the American Revolution.

20
GEOFFREY CHAUCER:
The Canterbury Tales

WHO WAS GEOFFREY CHAUCER?

Geoffrey Chaucer (1340–1400), the English poet, was also a civil servant and a diplomat. Chaucer was born in London into a well-to-do family of wine merchants, and during the course of his life he made a significant contribution to English literature by writing in English during a time when most court poetry was being written in Anglo-Norman or Latin.

Chaucer served the crown or the nobility, beginning in 1357 when, through his father's connections, he became a page to Elizabeth de Burgh, the Countess of Ulster. In 1359 he served in King Edward III's Army when Edward invaded France at the beginning of the Hundred Years' War. During the siege of Reims, Chaucer was captured by the French, but Edward III valued Chaucer's military skills so much that he personally ransomed him. Later, during the

150

reigns of both Edward III and Richard II, Chaucer held a number of positions at court, including the posts of Comptroller of the Customs and Clerk of the King's Works (the institution that maintained and repaired governmental buildings). He was subsequently appointed Justice of the Peace in Kent and was elected to Parliament. As well, he went on diplomatic missions to the Continent during the 1370s, including some missions to Italy where he may have come into contact with medieval Italian poetry for the first time. It is even possible that in 1372 he met Petrarch or even Giovanni Boccaccio, the Italian humanist poet who was Petrarch's friend. Critics have noted that Chaucer's own work seems to have been inspired from his exposure to Italian verse and Italian poets.

By 1366 he had married Philippa Roet, a lady-in-waiting to Edward III's queen, and they had two sons. After Philippa's death in 1387, Chaucer re-entered the crown's service. It was also a period of creativity for Chaucer; he wrote many of his great poems during this time, including Troilus and Cressida. Much of the inspiration for his work came from the poetry of Ovid and Virgil and the work of such Italian authors as Dante and Petrarch. Scholars believe that

Chaucer's early writings were also influenced by French literature: Chaucer could read French, Italian, and Latin.

Chaucer was buried without fanfare in Westminster Abbey in a spot at the entrance to St. Benedict's Chapel. In 1556, in recognition of his reputation as one of the great English poets, his tomb was moved to its present location in the south transept in that area now known as Poet's Corner.

THE WORKS

The Canterbury Tales

Chaucer is best known for his epic work, *The Canterbury Tales.* Written primarily after 1387, the unfinished *The Canterbury Tales* is a collection of stories about 30 pilgrims (one of whom is the impartial narrator Chaucer) who gather at the Tabard Inn at Southwark across the Thames River from Central London and travel to the shrine of St. Thomas à Becket at Canterbury. The pilgrims, representing a cross-section of 14th century English society, tell each other stories to pass the time on the journey. Among the pilgrims are a knight, a priest, a ploughman, a miller, a clerk, a merchant, and a wife from Bath. Many critics view the knight, the priest, and the ploughman as exemplars of the three estates of the Middle

Ages — the nobility, the clergy, and the workers. The other characters are drawn from the middle class of 14th century English society.

The diverse stories are divided into separate sections of one or more tales with links to intervals in which the characters converse with each other and reveal medieval attitudes and customs from all social points of view; common themes are love, marriage, and domestic harmony.

Chaucer's plan, outlined in the general prologue, was to have each traveler tell two tales on the way to Canterbury and two tales on the way home. Chaucer completed only 24 tales, four of which are themselves incomplete. The pilgrimage is therefore one-way.

Chaucer wanted to portray the pilgrimage as an intimation of the human journey from earth to heaven.

The significance of Chaucer rests not only on his skill as a storyteller in *The Canterbury Tales* but also on his innovations in its rhyming verse. Chaucer was one of the first English poets to use the seven-line stanza in iambic pentameter — the five-stress line — known as rhyme royal; as well, he uses the heroic couplet in his work. He also helped increase the prestige of English as a literary language and to standardize Middle English dialect. Chaucer was not afraid to write in regional dialects to improve the story or add humor. His skill in doing so makes Chaucer one of the earliest satirists in the English language, and his work later influenced the greatest of English satirists, Jonathan Swift. *The Canterbury Tales* is often considered the forerunner of subsequent satiric travel narratives, such as Swift's *Gulliver's Travels* in the 18th century or even Vladimir Nabokov's *Lolita* in the 20th century.

Chaucer's influence dominated the thinking and work of subsequent 15th century writers, but thereafter a major change in the English language resulted in a diminished understanding of Chaucer's language. Much of his verse depended on sounding a final e; it has become silent or has disappeared in modern English. Yet, though Middle English differs from today's English, most readers can, with a little effort, understand Chaucer's stories — often after reading them aloud. Many linguists consider the modern Scottish accent the closest to that of Chaucer, which explains the popularity of Chaucer in Scotland, both in the centuries immediately following Chaucer's death and today.

Many writers have imitated Chaucer's

style and techniques. Shakespeare borrowed the plot from Chaucer's "Troilus and Cressida" for his own play of that name. The comic and light humor of other Shakespeare plays also reflect the spirit of Chaucerian wit. The 16th century poet Edmund Spenser looked up to Chaucer as an inspiration and a mentor. Alexander Pope and John Dryden in the 18th century rewrote and modernized some of the tales. Dryden alluded to Chaucer's timelessness in his "Preface to the Fables" in 1700: "He must have been a man of a most wonderful comprehensive nature, because, as it has been truly observed of him, he has taken into the compass of his *Canterbury Tales* the various manners and humors (as we now call them) of the whole English nation in his age."

21
SIR THOMAS MALORY:
Le Morte d'Arthur

WHO WAS SIR THOMAS MALORY?

Nothing in Malory's life makes sense. How did the well-off knight become the hardened criminal who was finally in the poorhouse? And how is it possible that Malory could have written *Le Morte d'Arthur?* Such questions are unanswerable. Even more bizarre, all indications in his book are that he wrote the book while in prison or, certain parts were written when he was out of prison, then they were written while he was engaged in his criminal pursuits. Scholars believe that he began to write the book in the 1450s, concluded it in 1470, the year before his death. It was published 14 years later, in 1485, by the famous printer William Caxton.

Le Morte d'Arthur

Because this story is so unlikely, scholars have tried to prove that Malory cannot possibly be the author of *Le Morte d'Arthur,* but most scholars now accept that the criminal-knight was in fact the author.

Malory accomplishes two things in his great work: he brings together all the myths of Arthur and his knights, their adventures and love affairs, and in so doing creates a kind of nationalistic epic for England — as Ancient Greece had, via Homer, the myth of the Trojan War, or Romans, via Virgil, had the myth of the founding of Rome, or the medieval French, via Turold, had the myth of Charlemagne (though Charlemagne was a real, historic figure). Malory's work is written almost a thousand years after Arthur, if there was an Arthur who actually lived; Arthur and his knights are models not of men of their time but ideals of Malory's own time.

If there ever was an Arthur, he was probably a 6th century leader of the Britons, possibly a Roman, who joined with the Celts to fight the invasion of Anglo-Saxons; Arthur is supposed to have won the Battle of Badon Hill (the battle actually took place). He surfaces again in histories of the

12th century. Because nothing about Arthur is "written down" between the 6th and 12th centuries, Arthur was probably a folk hero, whose exploits were told in song or recited by storytellers. By the 12th century, however, his fame had probably also spread to France and northern Italy.

In 1137 Geoffrey of Monmonth's *History of the Kings of Britain* was published, and in it Arthur plays a prominent part; he is presented as the greatest of Geoffrey's mythical kings — and Geoffrey's work is essentially patriotic. It creates a myth that continues earlier myths — just as Romulus fled from Troy to Rome and founded the Roman Empire, so did Brutus flee to Britain and found that kingdon. Thus, Britain is, like Rome, a descendant of the Greek world, and the greatest of its mythical kings, Arthur, has virtues that rival those of notable warrior-kings of the past.

Arthur became the subject of what we now call the "Breton lays," French poems popular from the mid-12th century onwards. Sir Thomas Malory converted these lays, their Arthurian subject matter, into what we would now call a prose romance — and gathered into this romance all the extant stories of Arthur and his Round Table that were available to him — a remarkable achievement when one considers he wrote the book while he was a prisoner.

Arthur and his court, though, are no longer Roman/Celtic warriors; they are men of the Late Middle Ages, exemplars of the Chivalric Code — and thus Malory not only creates his national myth but also provides, within this myth, what he sees as a model of human behavior. Malory's world is one of moral behavior, courtesy to others, decorous conversation. More important, it is a world of Christian men and women, who believe in service to others as the highest virtue, for whom the greatest quest is that for the Holy Grail, the cup from which Christ drank at the Last Supper. For finding that Grail promises to unite the finder with the essence of Christ. It is a world in which Christian virtues actually exist, in which love is the highest of those virtues; love between individuals (between Knights of the Round Table; between the Knights and their beloved wives and mistresses) is an ideal that must always be upheld — as must the ideals of bravery, loyalty, and honor.

All of this describes the highest goals of Malory's world, the world of Camelot (a modern world synonym for a perfect world). But we, as readers, would not be fascinated by Malory's world if that world was one that had achieved perfection. Perfection, in Malory, remains the ideal. His stories are about the ways in which his characters fail to reach that perfection. It is a world of rivalries, of revenge and selfishness and malice, adulterous love affairs, of quests and battles that go wrong.

The fascination of *Le Morte d'Arthur* for modern readers is that it posits a perfect world, an ideal of human behavior, then shows, in stories that have lasted for centuries, stories that appeal even to children, the ways in which human beings always fall short of their own ideals. It is a common theme of the world's literature, but very few writers have presented the human dilemma as effectively and dramatically as has Malory.

22
Leonardo da Vinci:
The Notebooks

Who Was Leonardo da Vinci?

Leonardo da Vinci (1452–1519) was a man of the Italian Renaissance and a prime example of what we mean by a Renaissance Man — he was a painter, inventor, architect, sculptor, anatomist, physiologist, engineer, musician, and student. Trained as a painter, he nevertheless took an interest in a wide variety of fields, recording his observations and ideas in notebooks.

Born in the village Vinci near Florence (hence, the appellation "da Vinci" which means "from Vinci"), Leonardo was raised by his father and given the best education obtainable in Renaissance Florence. In 1466 he was apprenticed to Andrea del Verrocchio, the leading Florentine painter and sculptor of his day. Leonardo eventually became an independent artist and accepted commissions for paintings and sculptures at his own studio in Florence.

In 1482 Leonardo left Florence to serve the Duke of Milan; his duties included designing artillery (as a military engineer) and stages for pageants (as a civil engineer). He also continued painting and sculpting. He completed his painting "The Last Supper" about 1497 and began to produce scientific drawings, particularly of the human body. His anatomical drawings, sketched while dissecting human bodies and small animals, are considered the first accurate representations of human anatomy and physiology.

Leonardo left Milan for Florence when the French defeated the Duke. Because of his reputation as a painter, the people of Florence welcomed him, and his work began to influence a new generation of artists. During this period he painted the "Mona Lisa," his famous portrait of a young wife of a Florentine merchant. With this painting he changed the traditional technique of portrait painting by including the woman's hands in her lap, thus giving the subject a more complete appearance.

In his later years Leonardo lived in both Milan and Rome. As he grew older, he painted less and concentrated more on his drawings of machines. His drawings of flying machines, parachutes, hanging gliders, helicopters, and submarines were far ahead of their time and were themselves works of art with their detailed shadowing and illusion of motion. His study of the human body, both structure and function, led to his design of the first known robot and to an explanation of the functioning of the heart's valves, even though he was unaware of the basic facts of blood circulation.

In 1517 Leonardo accepted the invitation of King Francis I of France to move into a large home near Tours. He remained there as the king's guest until his death in 1519 and was buried in the Chapel of Saint-Hubert in the castle of Amboise.

THE WORKS

The Notebooks

Throughout his life, Leonardo kept notebooks in which he recorded daily his observations, ideas, and drawings. *The Notebooks* were originally loose sheets of paper of different sizes and types; they were bound together as volumes only after his death. The entries also include short essays and notes, all written in Italian and in Leonardo's mirror writing — left-handed and moving from right to left. No one knows why Leonardo never published his notebooks or why he wrote in mirror writing.

Some historians believe that Leonardo kept the notebooks as a private journal to prevent anyone from using his ideas irresponsibly, such as building military weapons based on his plans. Others think he periodically reviewed his notes to revise, upgrade, or add material.

Leonardo began the first section of *The Notebooks* in Florence in 1508, but the rest of the notes were written during different periods in his life. The work contains notes and drawings on a variety of subjects from mechanics, hydrodynamics, anatomy, and botany to the flight of birds. Leonardo was interested in the geometry of the patterns of light reflection, in the use of mirrors as sources of heat, human anatomy and physiology (including embryology and pregnancy), architecture, and painting techniques, all of which he discussed or sketched in his *Notebooks.*

Leonardo's *Notebooks* contain thousands of pages of notes and drawings; they reflect his approach to science and art. Leonardo did not differentiate between art and science but instead described or depicted an object or a subject in great detail as a means of understanding what he was observing. Leonardo was not interested in conducting experiments or formulating theoretical explanations; rather, he explored ideas and topics as a kind of brilliantly informed observer.

His *Notebooks* — in the form of loose pages and jotted notes — were distributed by friends after his death and eventually became part of major collections in the Louvre in Paris, the National Library of Spain, the Ambrosian Library in Milan, and the British Library in London. The Ambrosian Library contains one of the largest collections, the "Atlanticus Codex," which is comprised of 393 folio pages containing more than 1,600 leaves of notes. The British Library's collection is known as the "Codex Arundel," because it was acquired by Thomas Howard, the Earl of Arundel (1586–1646) and later presented by the Earl of Arundel's descendants first to the Royal Society, then to the British Museum, and finally to the British Library. The major scientific work of Leonardo, the "Codex Leicester," written between 1506 and 1510, is the only collection in private hands; it is on loan to major museums for display by its owner, William H. Gates, III.

Leonardo remains the prototype of the Renaissance man who was both curious and inventive. That he was also talented allowed him to express his observations in tangible and accessible ways. Although only a few of his paintings survive, his *Notebooks* have preserved the legacy of a man skilled and well-versed in the arts and sciences.

During his apprenticeship under Andrea del Verrocchio, Leonardo was exposed to many forms of artistic expression, including painting and sculpture. His abilities in painting, however, took him beyond the lessons of his teacher. He developed new painting techniques in many of his own pieces. He conceived of and perfected a color technique known as "chiaroscuro," using his own custom-made paints to portray subtle transitions between color areas to emphasize contrast between light and dark. He also developed a technique known as "sfumato," which creates a hazy or smoky effect.

In science and engineering, Leonardo's ideas were far ahead of his time. His fascination with aviation led to his detailed notes and drawings of the flight of birds. He used these observations to plan several flying machines, including an artificial bird, a hang glider, and a helicopter. He even designed a parachute. He designed bridges (his design in 1502 for a bridge at the mouth of Bosporus was the basis of a bridge constructed in Norway in 2001), a submarine, an early calculator, and a robot. His military designs included an armored tank, machine gun, and a cluster bomb. Presciently, given the current need for alternative energy sources, Leonardo studied and suggested industrial uses of solar power by using concave mirrors to heat water.

Most of Leonardo's devices and inventions were not constructed during his lifetime because the technology needed to manufacture the inventions was not yet available. His work did produce, however, in many instances, prototypes of many items used today.

Leonardo's interest in anatomy and physiology began when he was apprenticed to Andrea del Verrocchio, who insisted that all of his students learn anatomy. As his reputation as an artist grew, Leonardo was allowed to dissect human corpses first at a hospital in Florence and later at hospitals in Milan and Rome. Leonardo was the first person to describe the intricacies of the human spine and backbone and to draw cross-sections of the human brain. His drawings of human fetuses in the uterus, as well of the reproductive and urinary tracts, are especially detailed and accurate. Eventually, his interest in anatomy led to study of human physiology, and he was able to describe the flow of blood through the human heart, which inspired later scientists attempting to understand the human circulatory system.

Leonardo's wide-ranging endeavors greatly expanded the scope of knowledge in art, science, and engineering. His early theories and observations have guided scholars through the centuries since the Renaissance. He was more of an intellectual than a philosopher, and his approach was naturalistic and pragmatic. His need to describe and draw his thoughts and observations have left a legacy of valuable knowledge to which subsequent artists, scientists, and thinkers have turned for instruction and inspiration.

23
SIR THOMAS MORE:
Utopia

WHO WAS SIR THOMAS MORE?

Thomas More (1478–1535) was an English writer, humanist scholar, lawyer, and politician. Because of his association with Henry VIII, he became an extremely influential and powerful figure in English Renaissance politics and humanism. Yet his fall from favor was equally dramatic and significant. His refusal to accept the king as head of the English church established More as a symbol of the individual who places personal conscience above the claims of secular authority. For his stance, More was beheaded by Henry VIII in 1535. Four hundred years later, in 1935, the Roman Catholic Church declared him a saint.

More was born in London, the son of a lawyer. After serving as a page in the service of the Archbishop of Canterbury, More attended Oxford University where he learned Latin and logic. He then studied law with his father and became a barrister in 1501. He considered joining the Franciscan order but instead decided to marry and start a family. He married Jane Colt with whom he had four children; after her death he married a widow with one daughter. He maintained his devotion to Catholicism and observed religious practices in his daily life.

More began his political career as Under-Sheriff of London in 1510. By 1518 he had entered the service of Henry VIII as councilor and ambassador, and after being knighted he became Under-Treasurer in 1521, Speaker of the House of Commons in 1523 (where he established the parliamentary privilege of free speech), and Chancellor of the Duchy of Lancaster from 1525 to 1529. When Henry dismissed Cardinal Wolsey in 1529, More became the first layman to hold the position of Lord Chancellor.

At this time, Henry was battling the Roman Catholic Church because he wanted to divorce Catherine of Aragon so that he could marry Anne Boleyn. More resigned because he would not support the king against the pope. In 1534 Henry imprisoned More for refusing to swear to the Oath of Supremacy, the forerunner of a law called the Act of Succession. The Oath asserted that Henry VIII ranked above all foreign rulers, including the pope. More was convicted of high treason, and he was beheaded. More's execution signaled not only the end of Henry VIII's endorsement of humanist principles and thought but also the temporary end of the humanist movement in England.

More's first language for his writing was Latin. His most famous work, *Utopia,* was written in Latin and not translated into English until 1551, years after his death. More did contribute to the growing body of literature in English by writing many of his religious works in English, beginning with his "Dialogues," which were refutations of the principles of the Protestant Reformation. The "Dialogues," including his "Dialogue of Comfort Against Tribulation," written in prison while he was awaiting execution, are important in English literature because of More's use of colloquial English. Despite his scholarly rhetoric, More was comfortable using humor in his written colloquial English, which added interest to his intellectual analyses of issues and his polemics.

THE WORKS

Utopia

Utopia was written as a rational critique of English society, as a satire on unrealistic idealism, and as a proposal for an alternative social organization. More coined the title from the Greek roots meaning "not a place" (ou, "not," and topos, place). His readers were to understand that More was employing the humanist's love of irony and paradox. He carried out the irony by avoiding blatant criticism; rather, his protagonists praise Utopian values, thus criticizing More's England by means of negative comparison.

The work is a narration by a traveler, Raphael Hythloday, about his trip to Utopia. As part of his story, he relates the customs and culture of this mythical land. More compared Utopian values — lack of poverty, simple legal code, humane punishments, unselfishness, and abolition of private property — to those of the English social structure, which by contrast he deemed inferior. In Utopia:

- Everyone works everyday to produce food to feed the entire population.
- All activities and social needs, such as caring for the sick and providing fam-

ily needs, are supervised.
- Money and valuable artifacts are meaningless.
- Laws and lawyers are not needed.
- War is to be avoided.
- Everyone is attuned to doing what is necessary for the greater good of all.
- Everyone worships a single God.
- Everyone believes in the immortality of the soul and life after death.
- Elimination of private property is the foundation of the society.

It is evident that the cultural values of More's *Utopia* are based on the monastic life, an established way of life at that time despite the humanistic and religious reformation movement. Despite his humanist philosophy, More was a product of orthodox Christian beliefs and a proponent of religious authority. His steadfast religious convictions in the face of his imprisonment and death are proof of his Christian principles.

More has influenced social thinking in the centuries following the appearance of his most famous work. The significance of *Utopia* extends far beyond 16th century England. More's *Utopia* has attracted modern socialists who find More a shrewd observer of economic and social exploitation. Thus, *Utopia* became an important historical reference for the development of early socialist ideas.

Many scholars have speculated that such thinkers as Thomas Hobbes ("Leviathan," 1660), John Locke ("An Essay Concerning Human Understanding," 1699), Thomas Jefferson (U.S. "Declaration of Independence," 1776), Thomas Paine ("The Rights of Man," 1791) and Karl Marx and Friedrich Engels ("The Communist Manifesto," 1848) may have been influenced by More's vision in *Utopia*. The American transcendentalist Henry David Thoreau may have conceived his own philosophy as set forth in "Walden" after studying More's *Utopia*.

Actual events that occurred in the years following the publication of *Utopia* may have received their impetus from the core idea of More's work: The change from a poorly functioning culture to a society working on more rational, egalitarian values. These events include the English Civil Wars of 1642 to 1660, the American Revolution of 1776, the French Revolution of 1789, and the revolt of the Spanish Colonies (Haiti, Venezuela, Colombia, Ecuador, Chile) during the 18th and 19th centuries.

Beyond its social and political impact, *Utopia* may also be considered an early forerunner of the modern novel. *Utopia* is prose fiction that supposedly propounds historical truth, yet its satirical tone informs the reader that is it neither real nor true. *Utopia* is a travelogue, a story, a history, and a satire, all of which are elements of the modern novel. More's skillful use of English vernacular and humor further contribute to the genesis of what has evolved as modern fiction.

24
MARTIN LUTHER:
The 95 Theses

WHO WAS MARTIN LUTHER?

It can truly be said of Martin Luther, as it can be said of few other people, that he changed the course of Western civilization. It is also true, however, that many people misinterpret what he actually did. Luther did not intend to found a new kind of Christian church. The concepts we associate with him — "Protestant" or "Reformation" — should really be appreciated for their simplest meaning: to protest, to reform.

Martin Luther was a Roman Catholic priest, who protested against his church, who tried to reform it; he did not imagine himself to be creating, founding, a new religion.

Luther was born in Eisleben, Germany to a family that had been peasants. His father had first worked in copper mines, later he operated such mines — we would say that he had moved from being a working-class man to being a middle-class man. In common with other such self-made men, Luther's father wanted him to have a better beginning than he himself had, and Luther was sent to the University of Erfurt, where he earned both a B.A. and M.A.; he then entered law school at Erfurt. In 1505, at the age of 22, he went through a life-changing experience: he was caught in a violent thunderstorm, prayed to St. Anna that if he managed to avoid the horrendous lightning of this storm, he would become a monk. Because his life was spared, he left law school, and entered Erfurt's Augustinian monastery in 1507. Luther was a dedicated monk, and in 1507 he was also ordained a priest. In 1508 he began teaching theology at the University of Wittenberg. In 1512, he was awarded a Doctor of Theology degree, then was made a member of the Wittenberg Theological Faculty Senate, a position he was thereafter to retain for the rest of his life.

THE WORKS

The 95 Theses

Luther was a priest of the Roman Catholic Church — he was, as well, one of its most prominent theologians and teachers. It was his study and research as an academic that caused him to begin to question some articles of dogma of his Church.

As a result of his study, Luther came to feel that the Church had lost sight of, had been diverted away from, some of the central truths of Christianity. The most important of his conclusions — in terms of his future and that of his church — was that, in his view, the Church had over time created a hierarchy of regulations and procedures designed to lead man to God. Yet, in Luther's view, *The Bible* promised that salvation is a gift from God, through His son Jesus — and that that condition of grace, man's preparedness for salvation, can be and should be achieved by man on his own. Luther came to feel that God offers salvation to each individual, that this gift depends on the individual's relation to God through that agency of God that man can understand, namely Jesus Christ.

It was a short step from this point of view to Luther's questioning the legitimacy of the Pope (God's chosen spokesman on Earth, in the view of his Church) and his priests, special individuals (ordained sacramentally) who could guide man, absolve him of sin — only priests, guided by bishops, in turn guided by the Pope, could bring a person to God. Luther came more and more to believe in a direct relation between man and his creator, a relation that had nothing to do with intermediaries.

As well, he questioned the legitimacy of the sacraments, particularly the Eucharist or Communion. Was Communion really an occasion of transubstantiation, in which priests (and priests only) participated in a mystical union with Christ, therefore with God. Or was Communion designed for all men, to renew their allegiance to Christ? It is only Christ, not the priesthood, Luther felt, who can reveal God to mankind.

In addition to his classes as a professor, Luther also was a preacher at Wittenberg's City Church, St. Mary's; as well, he was now and then asked to preach to Wittenberg's Elector and his court at the Castle Church. In all of these activities as speaker, his new views had emerged — yet it was the question of indulgences that brought matters to a head. An "indulgence" was supposed to remove any sin that still remained after absolution — a forgiveness on earth, as well a forgiveness for souls in Purgatory; they were sold by the Church as a way of raising funds. Luther saw this trade as one that could mislead people — they would rely on paying their way out of sin, rather than truly repenting. In 1516 and 1517 he preached three sermons against this practice, then, on October 13, 1517, he posted *The 95 Theses* on the door of the Castle Church in Wittenberg. In his *Theses* Luther is actually rather mild — he condemns greed and worldliness in the Church and he asks for further study of what the sellers of indulgences should be allowed to claim.

But the floodgates were open. However unobtrusively, Luther, a priest, had questioned the Church. Within 2 weeks copies of *The 95 Theses* had spread throughout Germany; within 2 months copies were available throughout Europe. Christianity would never be the same again.

The rest of Luther's life was one of conflict. The Pope got involved, ordered one of his advisers to look into the matter of the *Theses.* This adviser declared Luther a heretic, and denounced his writing and preaching. Luther responded with equal determination, and a heated controversy developed, with Luther's eventually declaring that the papacy had nothing to do with the actuality of Christianity — that the "keys to the kingdom" had been given not to one man but to all of the faithful. In all of this, Luther's fame grew, and students and scholars flocked to Wittenberg to hear

Luther preach on what he regarded as the corruption and false teaching of the papacy; instead, Luther emphasized the supreme worth of the individual's relation not to his spiritual advisers but to God. One of his most famous phrases of the time was: "I submit to no laws of interpreting the Word of God." The inevitable took place; 3 years after Luther had posted The *95 Theses,* the Pope excommunicated him.

The Holy Roman Emperor then got involved. Charles V opened the imperial Diet of Worms in January 1521, and Luther was summoned there to renounce his views. Luther testified and said: "I do not accept the authority of popes and councils — my conscience is captive to the Word of God." Again, the inevitable happened — Luther was declared an outlaw and a heretic, and his writings were banned. Luther was exiled for a year to Wartburg Castle, where he worked on a translation of the *New Testament* into German, a feat that later directly influenced the *King James Bible.* Such a task also involved a concentrated study of *The Bible,* his earlier study of which had provoked so many of his ideas.

For the rest of his life Luther continued to refine those ideas — for example: The ordination of a priest is not a sacrament; it is simply an acknowledgement that someone has been "called" to the service of preaching and administering the sacraments to his fellow mortals.

Whether Luther ever thought of himself as a radical, founding a new church, is open to question. But, in the end, his views were sufficiently divergent from those of the Church, which early in his life he had served, that congregations, accepting his views, began to form even during his own lifetime. Whatever his intentions, a new Church did continue to come into being. 70 million Christians now call themselves Lutherans, and in the world today there are some 400 million Christians who call themselves Protestants, who trace their history back to Martin Luther. We should all remember that it was *The 95 Theses* that started this phenomenon that changed our civilization — but we should as well remember, whatever our religion affiliations, that Luther's message was at its most basic one that was both simple and that relied on the individual. Luther felt, finally, that man should not live in some kind of spiritual slavery to his own sins, particularly those sins that someone else defined for him, but should instead attempt to live a life of love and service to others. It is a notion that in its time was revolutionary, but readers should remember that it is also a message, whatever its effect, that is truly benign and, in the end, spiritual.

25
MICHEL DE MONTAIGNE:
Essays

WHO WAS MICHEL DE MONTAIGNE?

Michel de Montaigne is an important and influential writer of the French Renaissance (he lived in the 16th century: 1533–1592). He is the epitome of what we now call the Renaissance Man — he was active as a statesman; he was a scholar and writer; he was interested in a wide variety of subjects.

Montaigne was also what we would now call "privileged." He was born in Perigord, in the family castle, not far from Bordeaux; his family was very rich. Not much is known about his mother, but his father, himself an interesting figure, was an important influence in Montaigne's life. His father served as a soldier; he also served as mayor of Bordeaux; and he had some very liberal notions of education. Montaigne was tutored at home (by a tutor instructed to speak only in Latin), very much according to his father's notions of "home schooling;" he then attended the best boarding school in Bordeaux, then studied law in Toulouse and became a lawyer. From 1557, he served as "counselor" to the Parliament in Bordeaux; from 1561–63 he was employed at the court of King Charles IX. During this period and after he also translated the *Theologia* of the Spanish monk Sebond, and prepared an edition of the works of his friend Boetie.

On his father's death, Montaigne inherited the castle (Chateau de Montaigne) and he moved back there in 1570. In 1571, at the age of 38, he retired from public life; he moved into the Tower of the Chateau de Montaigne, and for nearly 10 years he worked on his *Essays* (in French: *Essais*). After living like a hermit for all of these years, Montaigne published the result of his work, his *Essays,* in 1580. Thereafter, he seems to have gone back, rather easily, to his life as a public man: he traveled throughout the Continent from 1580–1581; while visiting Rome in 1581 he learned that he had been elected Mayor of Bordeaux; he returned there and served until 1585. Thereafter, he continued to revise and expand and oversee the publication of his *Essays* — until his death in 1592.

THE WORKS

Essays

Montaigne seems to have been that very rare kind of individual who can both pursue a public/professional life at the same time that he can step away from that life and create an enduring work of literary art.

But his accomplishment is not just in his life but in his art itself. Montaigne is credited with almost single-handedly having created the literary form of the essay, with influencing writers and philosophers who came after him (including people as diverse as Shakespeare and Nietzsche), and, with his *Essays,* of having established a tone and method of literary non-fiction that is still the accepted standard even now. Every memoir, biography, autobiography, collections of essays or articles now being published bears his stamp.

His accomplishment was not just the form but what he managed to encompass within that form. He combined the personal with the objective; in his work, casual ruminations co-exist with intellectual speculation. In his own time, Montaigne, revered as a statesman and abitrator (particularly of conflicts between Catholics and Protestants and between adherents of one royal faction against the other), was not greatly honored as a writer. People of his own time were confused by what they saw as the lack of the formal in his work. It seemed too personal. Montaigne himself said: "I am the matter of my book" — in other words, I am my own subject. To a 16th century Frenchman, such an attitude was very strange indeed — non-serious, even self-indulgent. The modern reader sees things differently. Montaigne expressed the thoughts of his age, its conflicts and doubts and aspirations, but he did so by relying on the only consciousness he thought valid — his own. Critics ever since have commented that his method (which has become the universally accepted method of literary non-fiction, which is why readers today find Montaigne so "modern") — makes him more honest, more reliable, more human than any other author of the Renaissance.

To have invented a literary genre, to have given it both its characteristic form and tone, and to have that form/tone endure as a standard for more than 5 centuries — these are great accomplishments.

Montaigne can, however, claim yet one more accomplishment: If we had to choose one authentic voice of the Renaissance — one that can best represent that time in history to those of us who live centuries later

— it would be the voice of Montaigne.

Most people know something about the Renaissance — that after the Middle Ages, a period of 1,000 years, a period during which most people accepted without question certain beliefs about this life and the next, the Renaissance was a kind of new beginning. The "reawakening" was caused by a return to the artistic and philosophical works of the Classical World, Greece and Rome, a world that believed in endless possibilities for human beings — for what they could know, for what they could achieve. The Renaissance was thus a period in which people once again thought of these possibilities — and this "new attitude" revealed itself in very disparate activities, from the exploration of the New World to the literary flowering of Elizabethan England. It was an age that imagined that anything was possible.

Montaigne, very much a man of his times, and very much the activist Renaissance man, yet steps back from the pageant, retires for nearly 10 years to his tower, and though it would not be fair to say that he puts a damper on the exuberance of his age, he brings a certain fresh skepticism to this growing belief in human perfectability or superhuman accomplishment. Is there a human nature that can be perfected? he asks.

He suggests that first of all we would need to know the most basic characteristics of that nature, and he concludes that, when looking at humans, all he sees is great variety and change — endless change. Moreover, he says, he can't even begin to understand himself; how then is he to understand others? And, if we all suffer from this human myopia, how are we to know of what man is capable?

Montaigne is not a cynic; he is a kind of corrective. He disdains man's pursuit of fame and riches; he wonders why man does not try to detach himself from worldly things — to prepare for the inevitable. He wonders: If we cannot even begin to understand self, how are we to attain true certainty about anything? In all things, should we not favor the concrete of our experience to the abstraction of our theories?

These are but a few of hundreds of examples of his thought, of the subjects of his *Essays*. In all of his writings, he strives to make man more moderate in his ambitions, in his expectations, in what, in life, he can achieve. His view is far from hopeless — he believes that it is possible to live a virtuous life, to live a happy life — but only if man recognizes the limitations of being human and understands that true happiness comes from contentment — not from impossible dreams.

Montaigne's voice comes to us from a time of "great expectations," and seems, in his quiet sermon about moderation, to speak to us now, just as vividly as he spoke to his own century.

26
MIGUEL DE CERVANTES:
Don Quixote

WHO WAS MIGUEL DE CERVANTES?

Spanish poet, playwright and novelist Miguel de Cervantes (1547–1616), best known for his novel *Don Quixote de la Mancha,* wrote what many people regard as the first great modern novel. Although he produced numerous literary works, his entire reputation rests on this one book, which brought him enduring international fame.

Born in Alcalá de Henares, Spain to a poor apothecary surgeon, Cervantes spent his early adult years traveling. After studying in Madrid, he went to Rome where he became acquainted with Italian literature. His life for the most part was one of hardship; one of the reasons for his travels was that he was almost constantly looking for work. He fought in several wars, lost partial use of his left hand in the battle of Lepanto, and after the battle for Tunis, on his return journey home to Spain, he was captured by

Turks and was taken by them to Algiers as a slave.

Fortunately for him, the Turks found on him a letter from the Duke of Alba. Because they thought that Cervantes was a man of importance, they tried to sell him for ransom. For 5 years, he was held prisoner before he was finally released. He returned to Spain in 1580, and 4 years later married a woman who was much younger than himself. During their marriage, they had no children, but Cervantes did have a child from another woman with whom he had an affair prior to his marriage.

In the years that followed, his life remained unsettled; it included temporary excommunication and bankruptcy. His plays, poetry, and his first major work "La Galatea" never brought him the financial security he sought. But life changed for him in 1605, when *Don Quixote* was published.

Although Cervantes was never made rich by his book, he did achieve international fame because of it and was able to escape poverty for the first time. He died in 1616, in Madrid, a year after he had completed the second part of *Don Quixote.*

THE WORKS

Don Quixote

Miguel de Cervantes is one of the most important writers in Spanish and world literature. His novel, *Don Quixote de la Mancha,* about a gallant knight "with the impossible dream" and his trusty squire Sancho Panza, has become world famous, as have his characters — even to people who have never read the novel. Cervantes is now well loved everywhere, but nowhere so much as in his native Spain, where his face currently appears on Spanish Euro coins.

Who was this man that could generate such respect from readers and endure through the years? What did he offer that other writers didn't?

It is generally believed that Cervantes wrote *Don Quixote* while he was in prison. It was his plan, when he conceived the book, to recreate the manner and speech of the times. This idea was then almost revolutionary. But since he was breaking new literary ground with his novel, he also devised many new techniques to tell his story effectively. To make his book "work," Cervantes put aside old story-telling techniques and created new ones.

One of his goals was to create a plot that

was believable and realistic and that would give his characters and story the feel of real life.

Unlike the books of his predecessors, his novel displays a mature skill at narration, dialogue and style. There is an excellent definition of characters, which helps make them distinctive, and there is even more realism and believability in his dialogue and plot than what was known in writers who preceded him.

The purpose of his book was to ridicule romantic chivalry, which was very popular during the Late Middle Ages and Renaissance. By creating a provocative character such as Don Quixote, Cervantes achieved his goal. Who will ever forget his vivid and believable portrayal of a man who, after reading many questionable stories about knights, decides to become a knight himself and "to right the unrightable wrong."

The general public responded well to his efforts to use the vernacular and to his decision to break away from the more literary style of the past, and they eagerly bought the book, making it a success throughout Europe. Thereafter, the novel became an inspiration to other writers around the world. Translated into many languages, the story of the gallant knight with the impossible dream has been adapted to many media — play, opera, movie, ballet.

Because of Cervantes's many sophisticated literary techniques, *Don Quixote* is not only called the first modern novel, but, as well, it is studied by students, teachers and critics for its style and seemingly effortless humor. Numerous writers through the years have been influenced by Cervantes including Charles Dickens, Herman Melville, and Gustave Flaubert.

Commentators have referred to *Don Quixote* as a prototype of the comic novel. Although the situations sometimes seem to mirror the burlesque in their attempt to create humor, the efforts are generally so refined that the humor never becomes vulgar. Cervantes manages to turn the action into something noble and polished by drawing on his skill as a storyteller. The 20th century French writer Dominique Aubier believes the book to be the first true modern novel developed systematically with structural skill. Unlike the disconnected stories of chivalric romance novels during the medieval period, Cervantes's story fits together well, and it goes beneath the surface of the characters to present in-depth psychological profiles. The reader encounters many firsts — a woman complaining about menopause, another character suffering from eating disorders. Cervantes even uses twists on character perspective to give an added touch of reality.

Anyone who has not read *Don Quixote* will wish to do so — to understand so much that has followed from Cervantes's great achievement.

27
WILLIAM
SHAKESPEARE:
Hamlet

WHO WAS WILLIAM SHAKESPEARE?

William Shakespeare has been called "the greatest" for so many reasons that readers and theatergoers may be forgiven if their heads swim when they come to his work. Shakespeare wrote 38 plays and 154 sonnets; as well, he wrote some occasional poems that are largely forgotten; the plays, and sonnets, are known throughout the world.

His greatness consists of these factors: He is the greatest playwright in English; many critics would argue that he is the greatest in any language. He is also the greatest poet and writer in English; again, many critics would say that he is the greatest writer that mankind has ever produced. It can be said of him that he refined the language of the Middle Ages, turned it into the language that the English-speaking world speaks today. In more literary terms, he perfected blank verse (unrhyming iambic pentameter — though Shakespeare does now and then use rhyme to close a speech or close a scene or to achieve dramatic emphasis); it remains the most exalted form in our poetic language.

In dramatic terms, he created a language that in itself creates drama — thus Romeo spots his lover Juliet at a window, and must tell the listener, the audience, his feelings. He says: "What light through yonder window breaks/It is the East/And Juliet is the sun." Shakespeare invents a language that conveys human feelings in dramatic terms, in terms of an action, an experience, to which the audience can relate. Then, as well, his reader or audience must remember: Shakespeare wrote not for an audience of aristocrats (though it is known that Queen Elizabeth I admired his plays, and he wrote one of them at her request) but for the common people of London, for whom theatre-going was a noisy delight; they did not always pay attention to the play so much as to the activities of other members of the audience — rather like a modern baseball game. Yet Shakespeare triumphed over that audience (all indications are that he was immensely popular), as he triumphs over us.

So great are these accomplishments, and

so unlikely that they could all be the doing of one man, that some scholars (for the last 2 centuries) have doubted that the Shakespeare we know about could have been the author of these remarkable plays — better known throughout the world than any other literary works ever created, with the possible exception of *The Bible.* Surely a more traditional kind of "literary man" must have written the plays.

Shakespeare's life provides ammunition for such prejudices. He was born into a middle-class family in Stratford upon Avon (in what is now England's Warwickshire). His father was a glover and a local alderman. Shakespeare probably attended the King Edward VI Grammar School, which, as far as we know, was probably a good school, if not Eton College. At 18 he married an already-pregnant Anne Hathaway. The late 1580s are known as Shakespeare's "lost period," because no one knows what he was doing during that time. By 1592 he was working as a playwright in London, also as an actor, and by 1594 he was part owner of the Chamberlain's Men repertory acting company. He was sufficiently successful as an actor/playwright/producer that toward the end of his life he was able to buy a house, New Place, in Stratford. He wrote his last play in 1613, retired to that house and died 3 years later.

Shakespeare was a modestly successful man who lived in the last part of the 16th century, the early part of the 17th century. If it were not for his plays, he would have faded into obscurity — as have millions of people before and after him. That the plays of such renown and brilliance came from so seemingly insignificant a man has baffled many scholars and any non-scholar who has seen or read one of them. But that surprise perhaps has more to do with prejudice than with solid reasoning. What the doubters are actually saying is how could an ordinary man, who did not have the benefit of a university education, who was, after all, a kind of itinerant actor working in conditions no more exalted than 20th century vaudeville or burlesque — how could such a person have created works that continue to astonish the world? The simple answer is genius — which stuns us whenever we encounter it, whether in the music of Mozart or the theories of Einstein. Genius happens not as a result of a university education or an aristocratic background; it just happens.

Hamlet

Even if William Shakespeare's genius is acknowledged, and even if his various accomplishments are noted, something in such an analysis seems missing. Why are so many people, centuries after his death, and everywhere in the world, still mesmerized by his plays? No ordinary theatergoer, encountering his plays, says: Oh yes, he refined our language into what we speak today — or, oh yes, he made iambic pentameter into the prime poetic form in English. Our responses are much more basic.

Examine one of his plays. Though other candidates have been proposed over the years (most notably, *King Lear*), *Hamlet*, among his tragedies, is generally regarded as his greatest play — if only because it has been endlessly produced. In theatrical centers such as New York, Chicago, or London, a year does not pass without a new production of *Hamlet*.

Does *Hamlet* itself convey Shakespeare's special genius — the one that goes beyond his incredible technical facility as a writer? And if Shakespeare is the world's greatest writer, wouldn't he have special insights into man's fate, the purpose of his life and of life itself; wouldn't he, at the least, have insights, given that purpose, into how a man should live?

To imagine so is to underestimate Shakespeare. It is very difficult to determine just what it is that Shakespeare believed. There are exceptions to that generalization — he obviously believed that, in general, people are selfish and greedy, that they desire to be powerful, yet power corrupts them, that their battles accomplish nothing, that their idealism often turns to cynicism as they have more experience of the world, that love is as likely to be destructive as fulfilling. Critics have tried to label him; Shakespeare resists them. His sonnets suggest he was homosexual; yet the very same sonnets suggest that Shakespeare, a married man, was involved in an obsessive heterosexual affair, or that he was a royalist — he writes about kings, yes, but they are always corrupt or being corrupted. Anyone reading any Shakespeare play is reading his or her own thoughts into it if he or she comes up with any "philosophy" of life that he or she believes is inherent in the play.

What, then, is Shakespeare's special accomplishment? It is this, that better than anyone else has ever done, Shakespeare says and shows: This is what is; this is the actuality of this particular human experience. He provides the ultimate "definition," not the meaning of that definition.

The plot of *Hamlet* — though, if presented in its entirety, the play runs for 4 hours — is quite simple. Hamlet, a Danish prince, is a university student; his father has died, his uncle has assumed the throne and has married Hamlet's mother, his father's widow. Hamlet returns home, to the king's castle in Elsinore, for the coronation. Once home, Hamlet is visited by the ghost of his father, who tells him that he has been murdered by the uncle, that his wife, Hamlet's mother, has committed adultery with the uncle — that the throne of Denmark is now corrupt. He enjoins Hamlet to revenge him, and, in so doing, to give peace to his soul. For the remainder of the play, Hamlet deliberates what to do, endlessly vacillates, is always in despair — so much so that readers have christened him the "melancholy Dane." In the end, he acts, but not of his own free will — he is challenged to a duel, which he cannot avoid; in that duel, he, his uncle and his mother all die.

Shakespeare is too wise to tell us what it all means; he is simply but elaborately showing us, defining for us, a common human situation.

Hamlet is not a nerd who can't make up

his mind. We learn that he is the ideal of a Renaissance man — handsome, gifted, fashionable, a good student, an intellectual, a lover of the arts — in all ways an admirable human being, someone others look up to. He is, like all young people, an idealist. Shakespeare says in effect: In all young and idealistic lives some event happens that shows us that the world is not as we had supposed, that it is corrupt beyond any expectation we may have had of it. And what is our response? It is depression; it is, more, the coming to a certain crossroads — what do we do to fight that corruption? — which question brings us to another dilemma. In his most famous speech, Hamlet ponders this argument: To be or not to be? By which he means: To live or not to live. He ponders further: If you fight the corruption ("take arms" against it), isn't your death a very real possibility? And don't we all try to avoid that possibility for the reason that none of us knows what death actually means ("no traveler returns" from that particular destination to tell us what the condition of death may be) — thus we avoid action; the contemplation of our own death "makes cowards of us all."

From the depths of his depression, Hamlet is rendered futile, constantly berating himself for not being brave enough to risk his life to avenge his father (save the world?). Shakespeare, with his masterful subtlety, is saying: So are we all such cowards; it is only in our youth that our own behavior appalls us.

But why should the idealist encounter the corruption of the world and be rendered powerless by depression, be tempted to "drop out?" Shakespeare does not answer that question. He simply says: Here is the definition of the Hamlet phenomenon; all young people, as they move from youth to adulthood, experience it.

Every play of Shakespeare involves this kind of definition — of particular human experiences.

To study Shakespeare, to watch and absorb his plays, is thus to contemplate these human situations — more perfectly defined by Shakespeare than by anyone else who has ever lived. To read or watch Shakespeare, therefore, is to define oneself.

28
GALILEO GALILEI:
Dialogue Concerning the Two Chief World Systems

WHO WAS GALILEO GALILEI?

Italian physicist, astronomer and philosopher Galileo Galilei (1564–1646) held the controversial view that the sun (heliocentric view), not the earth (geocentric view), was the center of the universe. In his book *Dialogue Concerning the Two Chief World Systems* in 1632, Galileo developed this view, and, as a result of his staunch position on the subject, he found himself in direct conflict with the Roman Catholic Church.

When Pope Urban VIII asked him to write a book on the two different world systems, Galileo was told that he should not in any way advocate heliocentrism. Another request by the pope was that Galileo should also present the pope's view. Despite this request, Galileo presented the pope's view of geocentrism unfavorably and his own view of heliocentrism favorably. By maintaining a strong support for the theories of the Polish astronomer Copernicus (heliocentric view), Galileo succeeded in provoking the church to denounce him. Heliocentrism, according to the Inquisition, was in direct opposition to the "Scriptures." Although most historians agree that Galileo didn't intend to oppose the pope deliberately, Galileo, nevertheless, succeeded at offending the man who had previously been his most powerful supporter.

For his actions, Galileo was placed under house arrest. While under arrest, Galileo once again defied the Roman Catholic Church, which had forbidden him to write and publish; he wrote another important book. This one covered his 30 years' work in physics, *Discourses and Mathematical Demonstrations Relating to Two New Sciences*. Because the church had placed a ban on his writings, he had to have this book published in a country where the church's authority couldn't reach, the Netherlands. Sir Isaac Newton and much later Albert Einstein both agreed that the "Two New Sciences" was one of Galileo's finest books.

Born in Pisa, Italy, Galileo was the son of Vincenzo Galilei, a mathematician. He attended the University of Pisa, where he was eventually hired to teach mathematics, but he soon left the university for a position at the University of Padua where until 1610 he taught geometry, mechanics and astronomy. It was during this period that he began to make scientific discoveries, the result of his own private studies.

His *Dialogue Concerning the Two Chief World Systems,* which was published in 1632, is considered his greatest book. It took him 5 years from 1624 to 1629 to write it, because he was frequently interrupted. The book is a dialogue with three speakers — Salviati, a Copernican like Galileo; Sagredo, a broad-minded man persuaded to Salviati's views; and Simplicio, a staunch defender of the Ptolemaic view (named after the famous Ancient Roman Ptolemy who championed the geocentric view of the world). Simplicio's simplistic dogma (which was associated with the pope) is keenly observed by Salviati. Because of the structure of the book, Galileo was able to claim impartiality; in reality he had weighed the argument toward the Copernican view.

In 1646, 4 years after the publication of "Two New Sciences," Galileo died. Although he never married, he had three illegitimate daughters with his mistress, Marina Gamba.

THE WORKS

Dialogue Concerning the Two Chief World Systems

It can be said of few people that they changed the world. That statement is true of Galileo Galilei.

Most people think they know something of the Galileo story, that he was an Italian scientist of the Late Renaissance, a contemporary of Shakespeare (both men were born in 1564, though Galileo lived much longer: Shakespeare died in 1616; Galileo died in 1642). Galileo was one of the great scientists in history, who advanced our knowledge, particularly in physics and astronomy — who, because of his insistence on scientific truth, got himself into serious trouble with the authorities who ruled the Italy of his time.

Ironically, given the almost universal acceptance of the story, this version of Galileo's life is only partially true.

Galileo was a native of Pisa, the first of seven children of what we would now call a lower-middle-class family. Because of his obvious intelligence, he was tutored during his boyhood, then attended the University of Pisa, but was forced to withdraw because he didn't have enough money to continue his studies. When he was 25, though, he was offered a faculty position there, to teach mathematics. That same year he was hired by the University of Padua, again to teach mathematics, also astronomy, and he taught there until 1610, when he was 46. Throughout this period he continued to study science, to make various important if not earth-shattering discoveries — but, apart from his great brilliance, there was nothing in this kind of life of teaching and research that was in any way unusual.

Galileo's quiet life was about to change.

In 1612 he joined the faculty of the Accademia dei Lincei in Rome, and almost at once he became involved in a controversy. The Church had become concerned about the theories of the Polish astronomer Copernicus. The most insidious of these theories, from the Church's point of view, was that the solar system did not revolve around the Earth; rather, the Earth was merely one of many planets and their satellites that revolved around the sun. The sun, not the Earth, was the center of the universe. Copernicus wasn't around to defend himself; he had died 20 years before Galileo was born. But Galileo took up this challenge, defending himself and Copernicus, finally publishing in 1632 *The Dialogue Concerning the Two Chief World Systems,* which offered the two arguments — that of the Church, that of Copernicus. The book is rather loaded; the Church comes off as absurd. Galileo was severely punished and ordered to appear before the Holy Office in Rome, where he refused to retract his beliefs. The court condemned him and his writings, and it forced him to retire, essentially confining him to his villa for the rest of his life.

What many people fail to realize is that Galileo's greatness may well be in the meaning of that life story — rather than in any of his scientific discoveries. Much of his scientific work is now known to be compromised. Copernicus, and his champion Galileo, were wrong in their rightness. True, the planets orbit around the sun, rather than around the Earth, but the sun itself is not the center of the universe — it, too, is in orbit, and it is one of countless stars in the Milky Way, which itself is one of countless galaxies in what we now call the universe.

Galileo did not invent the telescope — as many people claim. He refined that invention; it already existed, though he did invent the first workable microscope. The story of his dropping stones from the Leaning Tower of Pisa (testing motion theories) is probably mythological. He did, though, make a variety of useful observations in astronomy; he did advance study of the first and second laws of motion — but none of these accomplishments would necessarily have assured him an exalted role in history — or made him an inspiration to scientists and to artists (his life and struggle have been the subject of various plays and movies).

Why then is Galileo held in such reverence? There are three reasons:

Galileo did not invent what we now call "scientific method" — the notion that scientific advance involves the scientist positing an idea about the world (hypothesis), then objectively testing this idea through controlled observation and experimentation. But Galileo was the first great champion of this idea.

Galileo also emphasized, and demonstrated, that the language of science is not human logic (as Aristotle had insisted, and as scientists, following Aristotle, had long maintained) — but that its true language was mathematics.

The third reason is the most telling. Galileo believed that the proofs of science ought to supersede the dictates of Church and State (which, in his time, were virtually the same thing.) Galileo, we're told, was a devout Roman Catholic — he obviously recognized no conflict between his religious and scientific views. His prosecutors had obviously forgotten their Aquinas; Galileo, just as obviously, had not — that there are the revelations that come directly from God, but there are also revelations that come from a study of God's creation.

Galileo would probably be depressed, were he alive today, that the conflict of his time still exists today. Creationists today insist that the universe was created by God in 6 days (because that's what *The Bible* says) — and was created exactly as it exists now; man, formed in the image of his Creator, has always been as he is now. Galileo would stand up to say: The universe was created over billions of years; man has evolved over millions of years to what we see now — and this process is unending. The universe continues to create itself; man continues to evolve. Galileo would marshal the scientific evidence for believing what he does, but would not imagine that, in any way, the scientific view detracted from the glory of God. He would doubtless argue that it should instill in us a greater awe of the majesty and power of God.

Two World Systems will give any reader insight into this remarkable man — and to the basics of an argument that persists from his time until our own. As much as anyone who has ever lived, Galileo may be regarded as the champion of freedom of thought — who, by his example and quiet martyrdom, made us look at the human mind, and what we ought to mean by intellectual freedom, in a new and different way.

29
RENÉ DESCARTES:
Discourse on the Method

WHO WAS RENÉ DESCARTES?

French philosopher, mathematician and scientist René Descartes (1596–1650) played an important role in the scientific revolution that was occurring in Western civilization during his lifetime by developing a philosophical base for the natural sciences. Much of what he wrote profoundly influenced Western philosophy.

Each subject about which he wrote he approached "as if no one has written on these matters before." Many elements of Aristotelianism, Stoicism and the work of such philosophers as Augustine are evident in his works. His most famous statement is "Je pense, donc je suis" ("I think, therefore I am"). To Descartes, the most certain knowledge we have is what we know of our self or from our own mind. He believed that what we experience through our senses can be deceiving; the only thing of which we can be certain is that which we know from our rational minds.

Descartes was born in Indre-et-Loire, France. His father, who was a judge, enrolled him at 10 in the Jesuit Collège Royal Henry-Le-Grand in La Flèche and later in the University of Poitiers, where Descartes received a solid education in mathematics, law, and the classics. When he left the university, the only knowledge Descartes wanted to pursue was that which he would learn from examining himself or the world in general.

He said: "I spent the rest of my youth traveling, visiting courts and armies, mixing with people of diverse temperaments and ranks, gathering various experiences, testing myself in the situations which fortune offered me, and at all times reflecting upon whatever came my way so as to derive some profit from it."

The Dutch philosopher and scientist Isaac Beeckman was responsible for interesting Descartes in mathematics and physics, which led Descartes to think about ways of using mathematics for solving problems in physics. Since he found traditional philosophy and religion disappointing, Descartes believed that only logic, geometry, and algebra could provide the certainty he needed to understand reality. Unfortunately, though, the "certainty" learned through this method could not tell him what was real, for these disciplines all depended on hypotheses. For answers, he needed a new method of thought to determine the validity of the reality that he experienced, one that would provide him with the certainty that mathematics offered.

In *Discourse on the Method,* Descartes's first published work, he identified four essential rules for validating information.

Descartes died in 1650 in Stockholm, where he worked as a teacher for Queen Christina of Sweden. The exact cause of his death is uncertain. Letters, though, indicate that he might have been poisoned. Over the years his remains have had several "final" resting places. Presently his tomb is located in the church Saint Germain-des-Pres, Paris.

THE WORKS

Discourse on the Method

Change swept through Europe beginning in 14th century Italy, which allowed man to step out of the Dark Ages and experience a new world, a rebirth of interest in the classics. It began in Italy, with what we now call the Renaissance movement, and it reached its apex in France from 1515 to 1559. The Renaissance movement was followed in the 17th Century by a major intellectual awakening, popularly labeled the Age of Reason. It is generally accepted that if it hadn't been for the Renaissance and the revival of interest in classics, the Age of Reason would probably never have happened.

What made the 17th Century (and the periods before and after it) so important was that it was then that man opened his mind to new possibilities — new ways of viewing the world and the universe. Among the great thinkers of this time were such men as Nicholaus Copernicus, John Locke, Isaac Newton, Francis Bacon, Galileo Galilei, and, of course, René Descartes. These great minds began to plant the seeds of wisdom on which modern man has since built.

During most of René Descartes's life, a powerful change was occurring in France. The death of Henry IV was followed by disorder. This unrest would never have become so significant if it weren't for the Renaissance movement. During the Renaissance, man had started to move away from the old views of life and began to make new discoveries. But like all significant social and intellectual change, this one immediately resulted in the conflict between the old world and the emerging new world.

Descartes lived in this changing new world, dedicating his life to his studies, and he began to defy conventional thinking with brilliant new breakthroughs in thought and research. Much of what occurred in philosophy after him was a reaction to what he had written during this period. He developed four primary precepts in his *Discourse on the Method* that to this day many thinkers respect and avoid violating:

1. Never accept anything as true unless it is obviously true.
2. Divide a problem into as many parts as possible to make it easier to solve.
3. Arrange thoughts in a logically connected order from the simplest to the most complex.
4. Make conclusions complete and general, omitting nothing.

Any time Descartes had doubts he would immediately reject his hypothesis. A humanist who refused to accept anything on faith, he believed the only thing that we can know for certain is what we think. "I think, therefore I am" became the most important words in philosophy — and the foundation for everything that followed.

These words had their roots in the experiences of Descartes's youth. During his early years, Descartes spent considerable time traveling — and like a wise traveler he would test his experiences by reflecting on them. From these experiences, he learned and wrote. And in his writings, Descartes set forth the methodology for what would come after him.

Descartes believed that the only thing that man can know for certain is what he thinks and knows of himself. He believed that what we experience through our senses can be deceiving. By doubting everything, he was able to reconstruct a new system of philosophy from scratch. This led Descartes to believe that only man was capable of thought. Everything else in nature reacted to stimuli mechanically.

Descartes's refusal to accept ideas on faith might have placed him in direct conflict with the powerful forces of the Church. This notion is probably correct. The Church was quick to react with force to any resistance to current dogma. There is no question in some historians' minds that, when he learned about the persecution of Galileo, Descartes reserved his real thoughts, kept quiet. He delayed publication of his work, the "Treatise of the World." To publish it would have placed him in direct conflict with the Church. The book maintained a Copernican view of the universe, which was in direct conflict with the Church's view.

Historians now believe that Descartes sought safe ground, avoiding taking a public position on certain of his views, a position that would have endangered him. If this view is correct, then one wonders in what direction his thinking, in private, was actually taking him. What brilliant discoveries did this man of genius withhold to protect his life? Whether this analysis is true or not is not important. What is important is that his ideas set the groundwork for other thinkers who followed him to support or refute.

Many refer to him as the father of modern philosophy, one of the most influential thinkers of all time: every thinker who followed Descartes has had to deal with his stance of universal doubt and the methods it provoked.

30
JOHN LOCKE:
Two Treatises of Government

WHO WAS JOHN LOCKE?

John Locke (1632–1704) was an English philosopher and social theorist who was born in Somerset (near the city of Bristol) into the family of a country lawyer. He attended the prestigious Westminster School in London and later Christ Church at Oxford University. As a student, he read widely but preferred the writings of such modern thinkers as René Descartes to the classics. Eventually, he qualified in medicine.

As a physician, he saved the life of Anthony Ashley Cooper, first Earl of Shaftesbury, which Shaftesbury never forgot; he thereafter acted as Locke's patron. Locke eventually was a minister in the British government. As well, he traveled and wrote extensively. It may be that as a result of Shaftesbury's prompting that Locke composed his *Two Treatises of Government*.

These two treatises defended the Revolution of 1688 (which led the British to overthrow its Catholic ruler James II); as well, they firmly opposed an absolutist political philosophy. Locke's ideas regarding natural rights and government were then considered revolutionary, and, for that reason, his *Treatises,* when they were published in 1689, were published anonymously. They are often described as a manifesto for liberal democracy and capitalism.

THE WORKS
Two Treatises of Government
Virtually everyone living in the Western world knows that, looking back on our intellectual history, we can identify certain periods in which a particular kind of social and philosophical thought was dominant. Most of us know that the Classical Period (the period of the Greeks and Romans and their many intellectual and artistic accomplishments), was, after the Fall of Rome, followed by a period we now call the Dark Ages, from which nothing very much survives, except perhaps the emergence and domination of the Christian Church. That period is followed by what we now call the Medieval Period or the Middle Ages, in

which there is a kind of stirring of intellectual ferment, as the world begins to develop — in its trade, in its social structures, in its formation into nation-states — into the world in which we live now.

And most of us know that the Middle Ages is followed by the Renaissance — a return to a more exuberant life experience, based on a renewal of interest in the example of Greece and Rome, an interest in exploration and new experiences, a flowering of literature and the arts.

We also know that the 19th century is the Age of Romanticism — a period in which a reliance on emotion, on fresh beginnings, held sway. It is also, not surprisingly, a period of revolution — most notable in the United States and in France. In the 20th century and in our own 21st century — we lack the perspective to understand what intellectual notions are paramount; it sometimes seems that all of them exist simultaneously.

But what of the period between the Renaissance and the Romantic Era — that period that extends roughly from the middle of the 17th century to the end of the 18th century? Sometimes the 17th century portion of this period is referred to as "The Age of Reason," and the 18th century portion is called "The Age of Enlightenment" — but, just as often, that 150-year stretch is referred to, simply, as The Enlightenment.

Most people have difficulty defining what it was all about.

The Age of Reason is perhaps the better description for this period — for it was in this time that philosophers, intellectuals and other thinkers came to believe and act on the belief that "reason" — the human mind, rather than human emotions — could solve most problems, could provide a basis for how man should live. This notion permeated all aspects of human existence.

Even religion. Most Age of Reason/ Enlightenment thinkers would say that religion in the past had been based on revelation — that *The Bible* is God's word transmitted through his holy servants, that the rules for men's lives are given to us by God, as a result of the interpretations of His priests, that we understand God's will through the actions and examples of His saints. Then, the Reformation took place, with its notion that there was an alternative way of looking at the intervention of God in life; Enlightenment thinkers built on that concept. An Age of Reason philosopher would say God exists in his handiwork — that Nature, the visible world, is God. His rules are those that govern nature; our understanding of Him is through an understanding, via human reason, of those rules.

The primacy of the reason makes sense in human endeavors as well. Whether we are considering art or ethics — the way we live, work or create — reason, not the emotions, is what will take us to an understanding of the world, and from that understanding comes right behavior and right thinking.

It is in this context that John Locke can best be understood. He is a man of the 17th century rather than the 18th century. For a philosopher, he had a very activist life — as a student, as a physician, even as a minister in the British government. Such a life would have been considered entirely appropriate by Locke and his contemporaries. The intellectual should also be a man of action, examining (with his reason) the workings of society and the relations of men and women to the society in which they live.

Although Locke wrote extensively about money and trade — and is very much one of the founders of liberal thinking, whose influence extends to the present day — it is in his writings on government, especially in his work *Two Treaties of Government,* that he has been most influential.

Within the time of Locke's life — as a

result of the creation of modern countries, with the establishment of trade between countries, with the ascendancy of money as the means of exchange, with the wealth accumulated from foreign exploration and conquest — individual governments became more prominent than they had been before. Although there continued to be monarchies, it was during the Enlightenment that the modern democratic state, ruled by an assembly of elected legislators, came into being.

What, then, Locke asked, is the proper role of government, this entity to which we give so much authority. As well, what is the appropriate role for government to take in relation to those that it governs.

Locke's views will seem familiar to the modern reader — for the reason that they influenced the founding of the United States. He argued: We do not simply accept that man must endure some primal form of government — that we are barbarians who must be governed in some way, however inadequately, by the strong and the powerful. Reason says that a government is legitimate only if it receives the consent of the governed. That is, there is a social contract between a government and those that it governs — in which both sides agree about the proper role of government in their lives. That role should be to guarantee, in Locke's formulation, life, liberty and property (a formulation that got changed in America's Declaration of Independence to life, liberty, and the pursuit of happiness).

If such consent was not given — if government was imposed on people or if that government, once created, so much changed that it no longer reflected the will of the people — then the people being governed had a right to rebel, the right, in other words, to throw out one government and create a new government that did have their consent.

Any American — or indeed anyone who lives in a country that purports to be a democracy — knows this message from the Enlightenment — and should read Locke to see from which man's thinking such an enduring notion has evolved.

There is another value in reading an Enlightenment thinker such as Locke. In the world since the Middle Ages, we have moved from periods in which the reason is imagined to be paramount to periods in which the feelings are imagined to be the clue to a happy life. Sometimes, to modern man, it seems as if such periods, in the past, lasted for a century or more; now, it often seems that periods of intellectual sobriety move to periods of intellectual hedonism within decades (as the 1950s moved to the 1960s; as the 1970s became the 1980s). We should all know the basic principles of either stance — and John Locke provides one of the best cases for the power of reason — one that continues to be felt in every aspect of American life.

31
SIR ISAAC NEWTON:
Principia

WHO WAS SIR ISAAC NEWTON?

Isaac Newton (1642–1727) was an English scientist who has been described as one of the greatest persons in the history of human thought because of his contributions to mathematics, physics, and astronomy. Within a span of 18 months, from 1665 to 1667, Newton developed theories of motion and gravity, discovered the properties of light and color, and invented calculus.

Newton was born on Christmas Day, 1642, in Lincolnshire, England. In 1661 he entered Trinity College at Cambridge, but he graduated without distinction. Ironically, Newton returned to Trinity College in 1669 as a professor of mathematics, and 3 years later he was elected to the Royal Society.

Newton developed his theory of gravity during a visit to the countryside, where he had gone to escape the bubonic plague in Cambridge. During this time Newton realized that the same force that attracts an object to earth also keeps the Moon in its orbit. Newton realized that the gravitational force of the Sun holds the planets in their orbits, just as the gravitational force of the Earth attracts the Moon. Nearly 20 years later the English astronomer Edmond Halley convinced Newton to publish these findings. The result was the *Philosophiae Naturalis Principia Mathematica* (*Mathematical Principles of Natural Philosophy*), usually called just the *Principia*.

Newton's discoveries in optics and light were also significant, laying the foundation for the science of spectrum analysis. By passing a beam of sunlight through a prism, Newton discovered that white light is composed of a rainbow band of colors. This discovery led to his invention of a new reflecting telescope that enabled him to see the satellites of Jupiter.

After the publication of *Principia*, Newton began to participate more actively in the public life of his country. In 1689 he became the member of Parliament for Cambridge University. In 1696 he became Warden of the Mint and later Master of the Mint, a position he held until his death. During this time he joined the Royal Society council and became an associate in the French

Academy. After serving in Parliament again in 1701, Newton left Cambridge and settled in London. In 1703 he became President of the Royal Society and re-elected to this office every year until his death. In 1705 Queen Anne knighted him.

THE WORKS

Principia

The *Philosophiae Naturalis Principia Mathematica,* or *Principia,* is a three-volume work published in 1687. It includes Newton's laws of motion and his law of universal gravitation. During his undergraduate years at Trinity, Newton had studied Nicholas Copernicus's theories about the revolution of the planets as well as Johannes Kepler's evidence that planets move in elliptical orbits around the sun. Newton was also familiar with Galileo's basic theory of dynamics and with the writings of René Descartes. All of these sources were instrumental in his development of his laws of basic mechanics as well as those of universal gravitation.

In the *Principia* Newton states his three universal laws of motion:

1. Newton's First Law (also known as

the Law of Inertia) is that an object at rest tends to stay at rest and that an object in motion tends to stay in motion unless acted upon by an external force.

2. Newton's Second Law is that an applied force equals the rate of change of momentum.

3. Newton's Third Law is that for every action there is an equal and opposite reaction.

Newton was the first person to borrow the Latin word *gravitas* (weight) for the universal force he would call gravity, and he defined the law of gravitation. He also provided the first analytical calculation of the speed of sound in air.

Although Newton is probably best known for his theories about gravity, his other definitions form the basis of modern dynamics and physics. He began by defining "mass" as the "quantity of matter . . . that . . . arises conjointly from its density and magnitude." This formulation led him to develop a definition for "quantity of motion" (momentum) and the principle of inertia, which, in turn allowed him to explore force through the change of momentum of a body.

Newton's rational and logical progression through these definitions compelled other scientists and physicists of his day to accept his theories. Although there are basic omissions in the *Principia* (the dimension of time, for example), Newton's work did lay the foundation of today's basic physics, even though Albert Einstein's theory of relativity in the 20th century superseded some of Newton's findings.

Newton's contributions to science and mathematics are obvious: his laws of motion, his explanation of the earth's gravitational pull, his development of the framework of modern physics and dynamics, and his invention and refinement of calculus fueled the beginning of the scientific revolution of the 17th century. By showing that the motion of planets and other celestial bodies is governed by the same natural laws, Newton was able to prove speculations of earlier scientists, such as Kepler's laws of planetary motion, and establish the Sun as the center of the Earth's universe. His theories have been far-reaching and long-lasting.

Newton also experimented with colors and optics. He showed that white light inherently produced the colors of the spectrum when passing through a prism and that the result was independent of the prism. He concluded that colors remain the same whether they are scattered or transmitted. From these observations he decided that the prevailing refracting telescope would be inaccurate in that it would disperse light into colors. To solve this problem, he invented a reflecting telescope. Newton also developed a theory about the speed of sound in air, and he proposed a law of cooling that described the rate of the cooling of objects when exposed to air.

Newton's most important contribution to science, however, may be his merging of two opposing intellectual trends of 17th century science: the empirical inductive method and the rational deductive method. This synthesis of thought was the basis of the scientific revolution and the beginning of the Enlightenment. By combining both intellectual approaches, Newton provided the groundwork for modern scientific methodology.

This kind of intellectual pursuit also influenced the prevailing religious thought of Newton's day. Newton's rational proofs of natural phenomena provided an alternative to the mystical and unsubstantiated claims of Christianity. But that he did so does not mean that Newton did not believe in God. He diligently studied the Scriptures and what most people do not know is that he wrote more about religion than he did about natural science. Newton viewed God as the master creator whose existence could not be denied. God's intervention in earthly affairs was unnecessary; His doing so would be evidence of an imperfection in His creation, and what Newton spent his life proving was that the world operated according to certain natural, eternal and failproof laws. God's creation was indeed perfect.

Subsequent scholars and writers have popularized Newton and his discoveries. The story of Newton's discovering gravity by watching an apple fall from a tree is well known. Yet Newton's accomplishments are of a far wider range. They are summed up by the 18th century English poet Alexander Pope:

Nature and nature's laws lay hid in night;
God said "Let Newton be," and all was light.

32
ADAM SMITH:
The Wealth of Nations

WHO WAS ADAM SMITH?

Adam Smith was a Scotsman who lived in the 18th century, a contemporary of the Founding Fathers of the United States (Smith lived from 1723 to 1790; George Washington lived from 1732 to 1799). Unlike the Founding Fathers, or other great men of the 18th century who are now household names, Smith lived a somewhat obscure life. He was, for 12 years, a university professor, then became a tutor to an aristocrat's son, then returned to his birthplace of Kirkcaldy, Scotland, where he devoted himself to his writing for the next 10 years. He then was appointed the Scottish Commissioner of Customs, and went to live with his mother in Edinburgh, and there devoted the rest of his life to his new and rather easy job and to the much more difficult task of writing. Smith was a rather quiet intellectual, not an activist, and yet with one book, *The Wealth of Nations,* he changed the world.

If Karl Marx can be said to have defined and refined communism, Adam Smith can just as surely be credited with having defined and refined capitalism as well. Almost single-handedly, Adam Smith created the academic discipline we now call "economics."

Nothing in his life seems to suggest that it will culminate in such an accomplishment.

Smith studied at the University of Glasgow; later, he went on to Balliol College, Oxford; at both Glasgow and Oxford he studied moral philosophy. That seems a strange discipline for someone who would become one of the world's greatest economists. Yet, all of Smith's views are grounded in moral concerns — economics, for him, is a means of achieving a good life. While a student, Smith developed his passion for liberty, and it is this belief in liberty that grounds all of his economic theory. He became interested in "the progress of opulence," by which he meant the ways in which wealth is accumulated; as well, he thought constantly about what he called "the simple system of natural liberty." His interest was not just in how a man should be allowed to live but also in what would be the most effective and beneficial structures for his labor — both for himself and for the society in which the worker lived.

At the age of 28, Smith was appointed Professor of Logic at the University of Glasgow, then became Professor of Moral Philosophy the following year. Gradually, his lectures changed — he started out by lecturing on ethics and rhetoric; in time, his lectures came to have more and more to do with his ideas about political economy — which, refined, became the basis of his book.

THE WORKS
The Wealth of Nations

The Wealth of Nations is perhaps the most influential book on economics ever written. And therein lies an irony. The notions that it offers, revolutionary at the time, are now so much a part of the consciousness and practice of anyone who lives in one of the capitalist democracies that we assume that, in a sense, those ideas are self-evident, that they always existed. That is not the case. Although he often refined and built on the theories of other thinkers, Smith devised ideas that basically we owe to him.

Smith suggested that there should be free markets, not just within individual countries but in the world as a whole; he objected to trade barriers or tariffs of any kind. He believed that a free market — one not restrained by government — was actually beneficial — that people, operating in their own self interest, actually if unconsciously benefited society as a whole — by helping to improve the standard of living of all people. A free market was not, as it sometimes appeared, either chaotic or unrestrained: it regulated itself. An "invisible hand" ("invisible" because most of us are unaware of it) actually contrives to produce the right kind and right amount of goods and services. Say that someone is successfully producing a product. Because of that success, other producers follow. Soon, there are too many of that product in circulation; the price drops below any acceptable profit level, and some producers stop creating that product. If the same demand exists, then this now acceptable amount of product brings with it an acceptable price level. In this way the unfettered market monitors itself.

Smith also rejected the notion that "land" was the single most important determinant of economic activity and wealth; instead, he suggested that "labor" was more important. Another of his ideas was that some tasks are better accomplished if they are divided into component parts, and each worker works on an individual part of the product — what we would now call an assembly line, which is the way that virtually any modern factory or any modern office is organized.

Because unfettered markets and unfettered producers could lead to monopolies, Smith saw the government not as the controller of markets but as a refiner of markets. Government should control any tendency to monopolies; as well, it should be a servant of last resort to those who could not educate themselves, learn a skill — or were, for some reason, incapable in participating in free markets.

All of these ideas — now accepted in most of the world, those parts that do not cling to some kind of planned economy — come from this one man. *The Wealth of Nations* should be read by anyone who wishes to know how the modern economic world we all accept as a given actually came into being. If, as someone has said, all philosophy is a footnote to Plato, then it can as justly be said, all economics is a footnote to Adam Smith.

33
THOMAS JEFFERSON:
Writings

WHO WAS THOMAS JEFFERSON?

Thomas Jefferson (1743–1826) was born into a wealthy family — his father owned a plantation in Albemarle County, Virginia. At 14, when his father died, Jefferson inherited 5,000 acres of land and dozens of slaves. Although the plantation was later to become the location of his famous home, Monticello, Jefferson did not really live the life to which he would seem to have been destined. He did not live his life as a wealthy plantation owner.

Educated in the classics, he was enrolled in the College of William and Mary when he was only 16. During his 2 years there, he studied diligently and graduated with honors. He then studied law, and was admitted to the Virginia bar in 1767. Jefferson then went on to become one of the most notable politicians and statesmen that the United States has ever produced, culminating in his election as third President of the United States, an office in which he served for 2 terms. He was also the principal author of the U.S. "Declaration of Independence."

After leaving the presidency, Jefferson founded the University of Virginia: it was unaffiliated with any religion, and it allowed students to choose which academic discipline they wanted to study. Both practices were revolutionary at the time.

In 1772 Jefferson married Martha Wayles Skelton, and they had six children. She died in 1782, and Jefferson never remarried.

THE WORKS

Writings

All Americans know who Thomas Jefferson was; so do most non-Americans. We know him because he is the author of the "Declaration of Independence."

The inception of the Revolutionary War (the war in which the 13 original colonies fought to be free of British rule) really began in the 1760s and 1770s, as relations between Great Britain and its American colonies became increasingly strained. The tension culminated in the battles of Lexington and Concord (small towns near Boston), in which colonists took on the British redcoats — the army of occupation.

To discuss the increasingly frayed relations between what the Colonists regarded as the oppressor (Britain) and the oppressed (the Colonists), some of the more prominent Colonists formed the First, then the Second, Continental Congress, which in turn set up a committee to prepare a formal, written statement of grievances. The committee asked one of its members — Thomas Jefferson of Virginia — to write the document, which he did; he consulted other members only for their suggestions. The Congress ratified, and subsequently published his work, the document we now call the "Declaration of Independence," on July 4, 1776. Americans regard that date as the birthday of their country, the greatest of secular holidays, and virtually any American can recite by memory the first few words of the Declaration: "When in the course of human events. . . . ." Ironically, though appropriately, Jefferson died 50 years later on the 4th of July 1826.

Jefferson's fame is so great as the author of this notable document that we have tended to forget his other accomplishments. They were considerable. As a politician, he served as the second Governor of Virginia (1779–1781), as U.S. Minister to France (1785–1789) as the first U.S. Secretary of

State (1789–1793) and as the Second Vice-President of the United States, under George Washington (1797–1801), and finally, and most notably, as the third President of the United States, after Washington and John Adams (Jefferson served from 1801 to 1809). In each of these roles, he was an innovator. And often he did the unexpected.

Jefferson is also regarded as the founder of what we now call the Democratic Party. It was a Democratic Party we would not recognize today. Jefferson believed in an agrarian society, one in which power was vested in the States, in which the powers of the Federal government were limited — yet it was during his administration, and at his doing, that the U.S. concluded the Louisiana Purchase, which considerably expanded the size of the United States, essentially paved the way for the United States to become a commercial rather than an agrarian economy, and greatly expanded the powers of the Federal government. Like Lincoln, who is often said to be the first Republican president, Jefferson failed to uphold some of his own most cherished beliefs when he believed that the country's good was at stake. Tax and spend Democrat? Jefferson reduced the country's national debt by half.

Yet, even if we acknowledge that Jefferson is not just the author of what remains to this day the most profound statement of the American consciousness, and even if we agree that he was one of the very greatest of our early national politicians, we have still failed to encompass all that he was.

Jefferson was also a plantation owner, who created Monticello, one of the most beautiful of American presidential homes. He founded the University of Virginia, and, an amateur architect, he made it one of the most stunning and architecturally notable of American institutions of higher learning. He was also a horticulturist, a mathematician, a musician, an inventor and an amateur scientist. In other words, Jefferson was one of the most brilliant men the United States has ever produced. He conformed to the ideal of the Renaissance Man — a notion that had its genesis 2 centuries before he was born — the notion that a well-rounded man was well-versed in a number of subjects, that he had a very many skills, that he was a "complete" individual — a notion that seemed hopeless even in Jefferson's day, much less our own. The concept of individuals as "specialists" in particular subjects was already well established.

Jefferson was a writer for all of his life — from an "Autobiography" to "Notes on the State of Virginia" to the "Declaration" itself to his two State of the Union addresses to Congress. There is no particular magnum opus, however, one that the reader can turn to as Jefferson's "definitive" work. His *Writings* is a compilation of his various formal and occasional writings throughout his life; it also includes his other public papers and a selection of his letters, some 287 of them in all — it was published by the Library of America in 1984. Though it is not of a piece (it was not written from start to finish as any kind of complete, planned book), it is the most substantial and enduring evidence we have of the quality — the breadth — of the mind of this remarkable man.

In *Writings,* Jefferson reveals himself to be what his admirers have always known him to be — an ultimately humane man, who regards life with reverence, someone who regards his fellow creatures with generosity and compassion. *Writings* reminds us of who the best of Americans really was, what he believed and tried to practice, and, in so doing, it provides an example for all of us.

34
WILLIAM WORDSWORTH:
The Prelude

WHO WAS WILLIAM WORDSWORTH?

William Wordsworth (1770–1850), with Samuel Taylor Coleridge, was the poet responsible for launching the Romantic Period in English literature with the publication of their *Lyrical Ballads* in 1798. Their intent was to overturn the pretentiously learned and rigidly conceived poetry of the 18th century Enlightenment.

Born in Cumberland, England, in what the English call the "Lake Country," Wordsworth developed at an early age a love for the countryside and nature. When he was only 8, his world changed — his mother died. Five years later his father died. Wordsworth and his three brothers and sister were raised by different uncles. Many years passed before Wordsworth recovered from the loneliness that followed the loss of his parents and his separation from his brothers and sister. With the assistance of his uncles, he was able to attend St. John's College, Cambridge, from which he graduated in 1791.

Wordsworth married Mary Hutchinson, and they had five children.

Although in later life he was considered a recluse "nature poet," such admirers as the American writer Ralph Waldo Emerson would frequently visit him to talk to him.

THE WORKS

The Prelude

William Wordsworth is one of the poets of what we now call the Romantic Period in literature in English. His contemporaries were Coleridge, Keats, Shelley, and Lord Byron. Arguably, though, Wordsworth was the most influential of these poets, for it was his book *Lyrical Ballads,* written in collaboration with Coleridge and published in 1798, that truly launched that movement in literature and thought of the early 19th century that we now call romanticism.

Lyrical Ballads is an act of rebellion against the thought and literature of the century just ending, and the Romantic poets have been seen as rebels ever since. Bohemians, hippies, beats — every generation has a name for its own romantics and their poetic/social followers. Wordsworth was indeed rebelling against the 18th century. It was the Age of the Enlightenment, and, whatever the licentiousness of the time may have been, it had been a relatively peaceful century in which the primacy of the human mind had gained immense sway. The notion that the greatest thing about man was his mind, a mind that could solve all human dilemmas, was truly entrenched. Its literary expression in poetry was the classical formality of the rhyming couplet. The rationality of the age also took other literary forms — mainly prose, which seemed more appropriate to a rationalist time than did poetry, a time that was emerging from and reacting to the exuberance of the Renaissance. The novel as we now know it was developed, and the essay (never before or since so popular) became a dominant, if not the most dominant, of literary forms. In the poetry of Pope or Dr. Johnson, or in the novels of Fielding, or the essays of Addison and Steele, the rationalist spirit had triumphed.

Wordsworth specifically announces in the preface to the *Lyrical Ballads* that he is a rebel. He says that he will write poetry not in the exalted language of his 18th century predecessors but "in the real language of men." Moreover, he appeals to the emotions, not to the mind. Poetry, says Wordsworth in this preface, is the "spontaneous overflow of powerful feelings. . . ."

It is, however, as much Wordsworth's life as his work that creates the notion of rebel of a peculiarly modern kind — a social rebel who is a bleeding heart, who creates a literature appropriate for that stance. Wordsworth was born in the Lake District, a picturesque district of lakes and verdant hills in the northwest of England. Despite sojourns abroad, and residence for a time in Somerset, near Coleridge, he spent most of his life in this beautiful area, and it figures, as inspiration, in his work. His parents were both dead by the time he was 13, and he and his siblings were separated, raised by different relatives: his childhood was thus both joyful and melancholy. At 17, he went to study in Cambridge, was already a convinced revolutionary and in 1790 he visited revolutionary France and supported the Republican movement because he believed it represented the best hope for mankind. After graduating the next year, he returned for an extended trip around France, met a Frenchwoman, had a child with her, returned to England and a few years later produced the bombshell of the *Lyrical Ballads*.

This early life colors our view of Words-worth. But, there is another side to the man. Though it, too, conforms to our view of a certain kind of modern rebel. Disillusioned by the Reign or Terror and the rise of Napoleon, Wordsworth turned away from his original radicalism, married and was the father of five children, became a family man; became increasingly conservative in politics and religion; and at the end of his life served as his country's Poet Laureate at the same time that he was the patriarch of his local rural society. The radical had become the pillar of society.

But this, too, is a skewed view of Words-worth. His sister Dorothy spent a good deal of her adult life with him, and when they were spending the winter of 1798–1799 in Goslar in Germany, he began, at Coleridge's urging, a work that described his early life and his ideals. It was published in a few different and incomplete versions during his lifetime, but he continued to work on it until his death, and it was not published in its current and complete form until a few months after his death — his wife named it *The Prelude,* and today we consider it Wordsworth's masterpiece.

The Prelude, which many critics consider the greatest of autobiographies in verse, is a culmination of more than 50 years of intense work — it is also a great poem of human consciousness, taking as its theme "the growth of a poet's mind." In it Wordsworth details the formative events of his childhood and youth, which he presents as universals; as well, he explains his radicalism at the time of the French Revolution. Ironically, *The Prelude* was to have been just that, an introduction to a greater work, *The Recluse,* a work that Wordsworth never completed. What does remain of that work has been of far less interest to readers of the last 150 years than has *The Prelude.*

It is difficult to imagine Wordsworth's intentions — except as he offers them in the introduction to *Lyrical Ballads,* with his emphasis on "powerful feelings." It is obvious that Wordsworth is countering the rationalism of the 18th century with the emotionalism of his own feelings, and it is easy enough to see in his doing so a reflection of a certain kind of cycle in society and its shifting adherence to certain notions. Thus, in more modern times, the conservatism and complacency of the 1950s is followed by the emotional free-for-all of the 1960s.

Wordsworth is, of course, a polemicist, offering the case for the supremacy of the emotions, for our natural response to nature and the things of this world — for heart over head. But to come up with so simplistic a view of Wordsworth, his life and his work, pre-eminently *The Prelude,* is to sell him short. He may be recommending the contemplation of nature and the events of human existence over the contemplation of the events of a book — but finally he is arguing for an integrated personality, one that depends as much on emotional as mental response to the phenomena of life.

The Prelude is a corrective, but it is a corrective designed to create a more integrated personality — the French Revolution is after all emotion gone mad — and it repays every reader to learn Wordsworth's lesson once again — that the ideal for man is neither mind nor feeling, but an integration of both into a whole personality.

35
CHARLES DARWIN:
On the Origin of Species

WHO WAS CHARLES DARWIN?

Charles Darwin (1809–1882), the British naturalist, achieved lasting fame for his theory of evolution or transmutation of species, achieved through natural and sexual selection. Simply stated, his theory proposed that the "best" characteristics of an organism will survive and be passed on to offspring and become the dominant characteristics of the next generation. This theory became popularly known as "The Survival of the Fittest."

Darwin was born in Shropshire, England. As a young man, he went to Edinburgh University to study medicine. While at university, Darwin showed no interest in becoming a physician, but instead he focused his attention primarily on natural biology. In 1827, Darwin transferred to Christ College, Cambridge, to be trained to become a clergyman.

After graduation, opting for a life of neither physician or clergyman, Darwin signed on for a long journey of discovery, a survey of the coast of South America, on the HMS Beagle. Many of his later ideas come from his observations on a trip that eventually lasted for 5 years.

In 1838 he developed his theory of natural selection, but he avoided mentioning it (except to close friends) because he feared he could be severely punished for his ideas. In 1859, he went public with his theory — with his book *On the Origin of Species.*

During Darwin's lifetime, the book went through six editions. In each one there were minor changes; for the sixth edition, he made extensive changes.

During most of his later years, Darwin was often incapacitated by illness contracted during his travels. He died in 1882, and was buried in Westminster Abbey in London; he was by then a national celebrity.

THE WORKS

On the Origin of Species

The name Darwin (or the term "Darwinism") has become almost a code word in the consciousness of modern man. "Creationists," as they are now called, subscribe to a literal interpretation of *The*

Bible, that God created the world in 6 days, that he rested on the seventh (the day that both Christians and Jews call the Sabbath) — that is, that the universe, particularly life on Earth, has always been as it now is since God created it, that it reveals an "intelligent design," being precisely as God intended. Often concurrent with this view is a belief that the Earth is only thousands of years old, a belief based on various dates that emerge in the stories of ancient peoples that are contained in *The Bible.*

In comparison, Darwinism proposes that the universe, the Earth itself, is very old, that our physical world is constantly changing, that plant life and animal life (including human life) have constantly evolved from simpler beginnings. Thus: man was not created as he currently exists. He has evolved from simpler creatures that were themselves evolved from even simpler creatures. We would now say that all life goes back to a single cell.

In some ways it seems like an either/or argument — not dissimilar to the flat earth/round earth controversy of centuries ago. There is a crucial difference between Creationists and Darwinists, however — just as there was between flat earth/round earth adherents.

Those who believe in "intelligent design" do so as an act of faith — *The Bible,* such people believe, is literal truth. Those of a more scientific mind (they are not necessarily anti-religion) might ask: Why, if He contains within Himself the universe and time, would God, after a 6-day creation, need to rest? In other words: Isn't *The Bible's* rendering of Creation really poetic, really imaginative? Just a metaphor? In contrast, Darwin himself was a scientist, and *On the Origin of Species* was published after a lifetime of scientific investigation (Darwin was born in 1809; *Origin* was published in 1859, when he was 50 years old).

For almost all of his adult life, Darwin was a scientist — someone who examines the natural environment in controlled circumstances, then records his conclusions, then tests them again and again, to prove them right — or, if the evidence of testing does not confirm his hypothesis, then to prove them wrong. In all of his investigations and inquiries Darwin did not reject God — he was in his early life a Christian, thereafter and until the end of his life he was an agnostic — he rejected God no more than, later, Einstein did, in proposing his own views of Creation.

Darwin, like Einstein, saw themselves as

describing the world created by a higher power, the workings of His creation. Both men would probably say that they were describing a more stupendous Creation than that imagined by the Creationists.

On the Origin of the Species — a book about which it can fairly be said: "It changed the world" — is thus not in any way frivolous, opinionated or flukey — it involves the considered approach of a man who was, by background, by training, and by life-long work in his field, an eminently qualified and gifted natural scientist.

Because the book so changed our views of creation, of the ways in which all life, most particularly human life, evolved into what it is now, it should be read by anyone interested in the world in which we live; the book is surprisingly readable and accessible, even to a non-scientist.

In reading the book, anyone should remember that its conclusions (except to a few scientists) were revolutionary in their time. Darwin was proposing that individual species of life originate through evolutionary change, that this change is sparked by their adapting to the environment in which they live. He calls this process "natural selection," that any organism or characteristics of that organism best able to endure in its environment is the one to survive, that the characteristics of that organism that allowed that survival eventually determine what the species will be like in future (for example: If dark-haired people best survive in hot, sunny climates, then gradually the people who live in that climate will all have dark hair).

Darwin, almost single-handedly, established evolution as the primary explanation of why nature is diversified. A bombshell at the time, and for many years thereafter (evolution was not universally accepted by scientists until the 1920s and 1930s), Darwin's theories, and reverence for his genius, are now accepted by the vast majority of the scientific community — even by most of the world's religious community. All of us — whether we are on Darwin's "side" or not — should know *On the Origin of Species,* the most famous book by one of the world's most famous men.

36
CHARLES DICKENS:
Great Expectations

WHO WAS CHARLES DICKENS?

Charles Dickens (1812–1870) was a prominent and prolific English writer whose novels, during his lifetime, made him immensely popular on both sides of the Atlantic. His vast appeal to readers has been attributed to his social consciousness and to his literary skill in creating spell-binding and comic novels that were yet very serious in their attacks on injustice, hypocrisy and other social evils of the 19th century.

Born in England into a moderately comfortable family, Dickens received a modest private education. But this way of life ended abruptly when his father was imprisoned for debt, the result of the father's extravagance. Dickens was sent to work at 12 to pay for his lodging and to help support his parents. His family's condition changed a few years later when his father was left a small inheritance, which enabled him to pay off his debts. The family's sudden good fortune did not, however, improve conditions for Dickens. His mother's insistence that he continue working left him very bitter. But it was from his experiences growing up as a working boy that his concern grew for the conditions in which the working class lived, and it was from this experience that the major themes of his stories and novels evolved.

Later, while working as a journalist for the *Morning Chronicle,* he met and married Catherine Hogarth, daughter to the newspaper's music critic. They had 10 children.

Dickens's sharp criticism of the social and economic system of the 19th century in England won him the respect and attention of such radicals as Karl Marx and Friedrich Engels. The writer George Orwell said, "Dickens attacked English institutions with a ferocity that has never since been approached . . . the very people he attacked have swallowed him so completely that he has become a national institution himself."

Over the years, many writers have been strongly influenced by Dickens, including Thomas Hardy, George Gissing, Samuel Butler, Anne Rice and Tom Wolfe.

Great Expectations

Charles Dickens is one of the few writers, in English or any other language, who has been compared to William Shakespeare. Literary scholars might say that, like Shakespeare, Dickens changed the English language — established new words, new meanings, more than anything else guided the way in which we have come to express ourselves.

But few non-scholars ever think about whether writers have or have not refined our language. In the more popular mind — the mind of the general reader — Shakespeare and Dickens have other things in common. Both come from humble if respectable beginnings, and both had limited educations — which, particularly in the case of Shakespeare, has provoked speculation that he could not possibly have written his plays because he lacked a university education! Both men made slight jogs in their chosen professions: Shakespeare was an actor who became a playwright, who probably never gave up being an actor. Dickens was a journalist who became a novelist, yet also continued reportage for all of his life, writing for a series of popular and influential journals.

Artistically, there are more interesting comparisons: both Shakespeare and Dickens were superb storytellers who created memorable characters, and, making allowances for the difference between 15th and 19th century communications, both men enjoyed great popularity during their lifetimes. Shakespeare was Elizabethan London's most popular playwright; Dickens was, and remains, probably the most popular novelist who ever lived (to this day, everything he wrote remains in print). Although Shakespeare wrote in verse and Dickens wrote in prose, that distinction is not precise. Shakespeare usually writes in blank verse (verse that does not necessarily rhyme); Dickens often, in the midst of prose, writes poetry (his sentences "scan" as progression of some variant of heavy beat/light beat, as sentences in poetry do). Hence, Dickens often sounds Shakespearean. As if to complete the comparison: both men died relatively young, in their 50s, having created an immense body of work that still stuns the world.

Some readers, though, might object to such a comparison. Shakespeare (either reading his plays or seeing them performed) seems "difficult," particularly his language. Dickens, on the other hand, whose language after all is much closer to our own, seems highly accessible. He always tells rollicking good stories in what seems to be down-to-earth language. Nothing could be further from the truth.

Dickens's language is both florid and dense; and, although the use of irony and symbol is hardly unknown in the works of novelists who came before him, Dickens is the master of these modes and devices — and in this he is unique, that many of the true meanings of his novels are unknowable without reference to their symbols.

Dickens's novels, without a deep pondering of his symbolism, are pleasing to readers as stories. That is why so many of his novels have been turned into movies, why a *Christmas Carol* is adapted for the stage, at Christmas, in so many different American cities. But a failure to read Dickens closely, with maximum attention, fails to yield Dickens's deeper meaning and commentary — just as a superficial reading of Shakespeare fails to tell the reader what Shakespeare was trying to convey about human experience. Thus, in a superficial reading, *A Tale of Two Cities* is about an English family caught up in the French revolution, or *King Lear* is the story of a ruler with a couple of ungrateful daughters.

There is, however, one crucial difference between Shakespeare and Dickens: Shakespeare presents, superbly (no one has done it better), the different situations in which humans find themselves — the human desire for power, our propensity to greed, the joys of love (and the impediments to love), but it is extremely difficult for the reader/listener to discover Shakespeare's stance on any of the universal human experiences he portrays. Dickens, conversely, is manifestly religious, believes in a higher power; more important, he believes that good in life ultimately triumphs — as it had in his own. His father had been imprisoned for debt, he himself had worked in an almost unbelievably squalid factory, yet he was the most popular novelist in England, then the world, before he was 30, and that fame and popularity lasted for all of his life. He ardently believed that, if one avoided certain pitfalls, life provided abundant opportunities for self-fulfillment and for happiness.

One of his greatest novels — in its plot, its characterizations, its mastery of language, its extraordinarily subtle symbolism — is *Great Expectations.* Any of Dickens's novels repays study, but *Great Expectations* shows him at the height of his powers.

Pip, a young orphan, lives with his bitter older sister and her saintly husband, Joe, in the area around Rochester, Kent. He is hired as a companion to an eccentric local rich woman, who was jilted at the altar and thereafter lives in the world of that moment — surrounded by stopped clocks, a rotting wedding cake, wearing a bridal gown now in tatters. Miss Havisham's only other close companion is her adopted daughter, Estella. She is training her to cultivate her beauty and her accomplishments, to tempt men, then break their hearts. Meanwhile Pip becomes an apprentice to Joe, a blacksmith. Miss Havisham pays the fees necessary to reimburse Joe for his training of Pip — but Pip has been entranced by the trappings of money that he has observed in Miss Havisham's ruined and neglected mansion, as he has been entranced (as Miss Havisham intended) by Estella.

In the fourth year of his apprenticeship, he encounters an escaped convict on the marshes near his home — and helps him.

Years later — via a lawyer who also serves as Miss Havisham's lawyer — he learns that he has "great expectations" of wealth, and moves to London to take up the life of a gentleman and to continue his pursuit of Estella, who has been trained only to repulse him and make him miserable. He forgets his best friend Joe, spends too much money, eventually learns that his benefactor is not Miss Havisham (as he had always supposed) but the convict he once helped, now grown rich in Australia. In the end, Pip spends himself into bankruptcy, loses his best and most well-meaning friends, yet he is redeemed by hard work and remorse, by the love of those he has wronged — and by the love of Estella, who, having suffered as Pip has done, comes to understand how she too has thwarted and cheated life.

Within this beautifully constructed novel, Dickens weaves a number of his characteristic themes — but nowhere so intensely and movingly as here. The power of money, or the emotion of greed, to corrupt. The joy of true love; the misery of love thwarted or demeaned. The damage to the human psyche caused by obsession with self; the happiness to be gained by selflessness. The beauty of true friendship, the ways in which such friends can form a life to the good, contrasted with the damage that false friendship can do to any life. Above all, the possibility of redemption, no matter how far we have fallen.

Everyone should re-examine his own humanity by putting himself or herself in the hands of this master, and by reading *Great Expectations,* one of the great documents of the human spirit.

37
KARL MARX:
The Communist Manifesto

WHO WAS KARL MARX?

Karl Marx (1818–1883) and Friedrich Engels wrote one of the most influential and widely read political tracts of the 19th century, *The Communist Manifesto.* Marx distinguished his kind of socialism from that of others by claiming that his version was scientifically based on history regarded objectively.

Born into a Jewish family in Trier, Germany, Marx attended the University of Bonn, where he studied law. His interest, though, was really in philosophy and literature. During his second year, he transferred to the more academically rigorous Friedrich-Wilhelms-Universität in Berlin. It was here that he began to write poems and essays and consider his own philosophical stance.

Marx's thinking was strongly influenced by Hegel's dialectical method. Ideas, according to Hegel, are formed through an evolutionary process in which a concept leads to a conflict of opposites, which leads to a synthesis, which leads to another conflict of opposites, which leads to another synthesis. This process continues progressively upward until an individual reaches the highest level of awareness.

Marx took this dialectic and applied it to history, society and economics in order to explain the causes and developments in human society. As feudalism evolved into mercantilism, which evolved into capitalism, so will capitalism ultimately evolve into communism, he believed.

In 1842, Marx left university life and became a journalist. His political views caused him to clash with the Prussian censors. He moved to France, where he met Friedrich Engels who awakened Marx's interest in the working class and in economics. *The Communist Manifesto* suggests the path to take for the overthrow of capitalism by proletarian revolutionaries. In the *Manifesto* a course of action is outlined that Marx believes will bring about a classless society.

To achieve communism, the supreme end of a stateless and classless society, a revolutionary government must be organized.

A crucial passage in the *Manifesto* is this: "When, in the course of development, class distinctions have disappeared, and all production has been concentrated in the hands of a vast association of the whole nation, the public power will lose its political character. Political power, properly so called, is merely the organized power of one class for oppressing another."

In the *Manifesto* the authors write that the communist party can achieve its ends only by force. "The proletarians have nothing to lose but their chains. They have a world to win." The famous political cry of all socialists, which appeared in the *Manifesto* and on Marx's tombstone in London, is: "Working men of all countries, unite!"

THE WORKS

The Communist Manifesto

Virtually any adult who was alive in the 20th century knows something about the life and writings of Karl Marx. He is a famous political and economic philosopher, one of the most famous figures of the 19th century, one whose influence was felt more in the 20th century than in his own time. A Jew who was born in Germany in 1818, Marx spent most of his later adult life in London, where he died in 1883. He produced a great body of work, and almost any educated man or woman has read about his work-and-study vigils in the Reading Room of the British Museum in London, which, in the popular imagination, he seems never to have left. He is buried in Highgate Cemetery in London, a place of pilgrimage for many visitors to that city. Yet, despite this enduring fame, and despite the near legendary quality of his life and his work, many people assume that Marx is now no longer "relevant."

Although the Russian Revolution (the Bolshevik Revolution) of 1917 happened almost 35 years after Marx had died, it was Marx's ideas (and those of his colleague Friedrich Engels) that inspired that revolution and provided the "philosophical" basis for what became the U.S.S.R. (The Soviet Union) — as well as China under Mao, Cuba under Castro, North Vietnam under Ho Chi Minh. In the second half of the 20th century, it seemed that half the world was comprised of countries whose economic and political stance and structures were directly influenced by the precepts of Karl Marx. With the decline, then break-up, of the Soviet Union, and the increasingly capitalistic stance of China, it now seems as if only a few third-rate powers still subscribe to, or base their economies and governments on, the notions of Karl Marx. Those notions, the man himself, seem, like the Soviet Union, to have been discarded on the rubbish heap of history.

Although the influence of his ideas has obviously declined, Karl Marx remains an important historic figure whose pronouncements about politics, economics, and the historic class struggle remain potent even today. The historic figures he inspired — the great thinkers such as Lenin or Trotsky or Sartre, the tyrants such as Stalin or Mao — are now far less important than Marx himself, their intellectual mentor.

His great and monumental work is the three-volume *Das Kapital (Capital),* the first volume of which was published in 1867; the last two volumes were published (supervised by Engels) after Marx's death. Given the complexity of this work, it is usually read only by philosophers and by scholars of politics and economics. *The Communist Manifesto* (1848), which Marx wrote with Engels, has been much more influential; it provides an excellent and brief introduction to his thought.

Initially, Marx's life and work were in the service of what might now be called liberal causes in the classic, conservative world of 19th century Germany, then France. After a career as a journalist, speaker and revolutionary, and a year after publication of *The Communist Manifesto*, he moved, at the age of 31, to London — and it is there that he refined his theories. He was no longer welcome in either France or Germany; England provided a much more congenial atmosphere.

Marx is a much more complex thinker than some of his followers, those who call themselves Marxist, often suggest. As well, Marx is not as harsh and unbending as some people have painted him; he is by no means some kind of monster whose ideas almost destroyed the world. Socialism, after all, in which Marx was a firm believer, is a humane kind of economic organization/government — that everyone should produce as much as he or she can, that all of us should be provided for — so that we all have a decent life. Marx could be said to be, in much of his thinking, a radical humanist, someone who wished to make the human condition better for as many people as possible.

Socialism proposes that the production of goods and services should be controlled by the state, which will in turn guarantee this central goal of each of us producing to the best of his/her ability, of society's taking care of those who cannot take care of themselves.

What Marx brings to this particular mix — he did not, after all, invent socialism — is the idea that history has been moving to an inevitable time when the state will function for the benefit of all. He argues that there has been a feudal period, in which people sold (or bartered) what they produced as a way of acquiring goods that they needed. As society became more complex, so did its economic systems become more complex, ending in the capitalistic system that we now know — in which comparatively few people (with capital) control the means of production and the benefits from the fruits of the labor of their workers, who have no direct financial connection with the products of their work. Thus, say, a man works an hour to create some household good, a cooking pot for instance. He is paid $10 for that hour's work. Yet the man who owns the factory where he works in turn sells that pot for $30, which involves $10 in profit, a profit that the worker never sees.

Marx argues that this situation is exploitation, that, eventually it leads to incredibly rich factory owners and nearly destitute workers (the owner constantly devises more refined methods of production, often not involving human labor, which in turns leads to unemployment, which in turn means workers will work for less to avoid abject poverty), a situation that must lead to conditions of revolution, in which workers (the "proletariat") will, by fighting for their rights, triumph and establish a new kind of economic system leading to a new kind of government, one in which we are all the "factory owners," sharing the $30 among each other.

That Communism in our time produced such dictators as Stalin and Mao in no way negates Marx's thought; it merely points out that there are tyrants of the left as well as the right, murderers posing as benefactors.

Marx's abiding legacy is not so much a system that has yet to prove workable as an idea that retains its potency to the present time — that in a world that gives lip service to the idea of human equality, our existing economic structures do not allow for such equality; indeed, they work against equality. Whether in the advanced democracies of the West, or the barely existing countries of poorest Africa, the division of reward is obviously in no way reflective of any ideal of equality. Marx's lasting accomplishment may not be the system of government and economic structure that evolved from his work — but his forceful reminder that, as human beings, we ought to be able to do better — to erase poverty, to provide healthy and fulfilling lives for all people.

38
FYODOR DOSTOYEVSKY: *Crime and Punishment*

WHO WAS FYODOR DOSTOYEVSKY?

The Russian author Fyodor Dostoyevsky (1821–1881) made a lasting impression on modern fiction with his profound development of characters and his incisive examination of the political, spiritual and social conditions of Russia during his lifetime.

Because he despised mathematics, Dostoyevsky wasn't a good student at the St. Petersburg Academy of Military Engineering, where he turned his attention instead to literature, especially the works of the French novelist Balzac. In 1846, he published his first short novel, *Poor Folk,* which was well received.

A few years later, Dostoyevsky's world changed for him when he was "linked" to a radical intellectual group that opposed the tsar. While attending a meeting, acquainting himself with Karl Marx's idea, about which he knew nothing at the time, Dostoyevsky was arrested and sent to Siberia. This experience — his having to live in appalling conditions — caused a significant change in him. Forced to mingle with all classes, Dostoyevsky altered his view of the common man. That view enlarged — he stopped seeing such men as just serfs, now saw them as fully developed human beings. This realization was to alter his writing, freeing it of stereotypes and bigoted caricatures of the lower class.

After his release from prison, Dostoyevsky married and settled in St. Petersburg where he and his older brother published a few literary journals. They were not successful. When his brother and his own wife died, Dostoyevsky became depressed and despondent. He now found himself deeply in debt because of his unsuccessful business ventures and his obligation to provide financial support to his brother's wife and children. He increased his debt by gambling. *Crime and Punishment,* his most famous work, was written in haste to obtain cash to pay his gambling bills.

Whatever the difficulties of his life, Dostoyevsky had a profound influence on the writers who followed him. The list of writers inspired by Dostoyevsky is long and impressive; it includes: Franz Kafka, Hermann Hesse, Marcel Proust, William Faulkner, Albert Camus, Henry Miller, and Yukio Mishima.

THE WORKS
Crime and Punishment

Russia has produced more than its fair share of important writers, and its greatest novelists are Tolstoy and Dostoyevsky. Both lived during the 19th century, and, though they never met, they knew and admired each other's work. Yet, though they wrote about and from within the same milieu, no two writers could be more different.

Tolstoy is the classical master: he re-created the vast panorama of the Napoleonic wars in *War and Peace.* Thomas Mann called it the Russian national epic; the rest of us would probably call it the greatest of historical novels. Then, dazzling in his virtuosity, Tolsoy wrote *Anna Karenina,* in many ways the greatest novel of society, the intimate plot of which could have happened at any time and in any place.

In comparison to the classicism and perfection of Tolstoy, Dostoyevsky seems a wild man. He is very much a man of his time and place in history; writes mainly about dysfunctional characters; experiments as a writer with stream of consciousness; offers psychological portraits of his characters; and, given these extraordinary innovations, has been a great influence on the writers and philosophers who followed him in a way that Tolstoy has not. One of his characters says: If God does not exist, then anything is allowed; and many of Dostoyevsky's characters live according to this notion, which seems to the reader to be Dostoyevsky's own conclusion about life. It's easy to see how such an attitude could be embraced by such writers as Kafka or such existential philosophers as Sartre.

Often this has been the critical view from which Dostoyevsky has been approached — as the great if messy and disillusioned innovator who had an almost unbelievably profound effect on 20th century fiction and philosophy.

Some commentators have seen Dostoyevsky's fiction as a reflection of his life. He was an orphan by age 18; at that time he was studying at the St. Petersburg Academy of Military Engineering. He studied mathematics, a subject he disliked, and he increasingly turned his attention to literature. At 25, he published his first novel. In his youth, Dostoyevsky was a revolutionary hothead, and he was arrested and imprisoned in 1849 (he was 28) for supposedly engaging in revolutionary activity against the tsar. He went to prison, in Siberia, until 1854, then served another 5 years in the Siberian Regiment (a condition of his being released from prison). During this period in his life he abandoned his earlier liberal ideals, became an upholder of traditional Russian values; as well, he became a Christian. He returned to St. Petersburg in 1860, was subsequently devastated both by his wife's death in 1864 and by his brother's subsequent death, as well as by the responsibilities of meeting his own debts and those of his brother's widow and children. Crippled by depression, he began frequenting gambling parlors, the beginning of an addiction to gambling that would plague him for the rest of his life. He spent much of his later life in various gambling spas in Western Europe and in Russia, and died in 1881 of the complications of emphysema.

The events of Dostoyevsky's life seem to lend credibility to the notion that his dysfunctional characters, who are inevitably suffering from some kind of addiction — to alcohol, to sex, to gambling, to their own psychological proclivities — that such portrayals, as within St. Petersburg, a city of unbelievable squalor, are really a reflection of a life that, compared to Tolstoy's, was, much of the time, out of control.

Yet such analyses — that he was the Russian wild man whose chaotic but innovative point of view influenced generations to follow and/or that he was a madman whose fiction reflected his own life as jailbird or reprobate — though these analyses are hardly far-fetched — do disservice to the man and his novels.

It is well to remember that his experiences made him a traditionalist. The reality is that he approached the greatest questions of man's existence, did so by inventing, for fiction, new techniques to ask old questions — created, from what he saw around him, the psychological novel, attempted to create complete characters who could ask, who could act out, the eternal questions of man's existence and grope their way to answers.

Crime and Punishment is considered by many people to be Dostoyevsky's finest achievement. Such a judgment must be subjective: is it better than *The Brothers Karamazov* or *The Idiot*? Whatever the final verdict, *Crime and Punishment* is a very great novel indeed.

In it, Dostoyevsky considers the question, borrowed (with his own variants) from the philosopher Nietzsche, of whether or not an ubermensch, a superman, can really exist. It is a question that went on to haunt the 20th century and haunts us still. In Dostoyevsky's formulation: Are some people of so superior an intellect that the common restraints on mankind — its laws, its taboos — do not apply to them, that they may be allowed to violate those restraints because, in the end, it is their actions, and their actions alone, that advance the cause of civilization and the consciousness of mankind? Readers of 20th century history will instantly recognize the question, because it surfaces in widely disparate circumstances, from the trial in the 1920s of Leopold and Loeb to the coming of Hitler, his concept of the Germans as a race of ubermensch, and it culminates in the horrors of World War II.

Dostoyevsky ingeniously reduces this proposition to the banal. His plot is simple: Roskolnikov (though of a good family, capable of working) is a down-and-out perpetual student, who studies/analyzes/obsesses about the chaotic world of St. Petersburg in which he lives. Sick and feverish, he contemplates the possibility that he is an ubermensch, then embraces the idea, then determines that he will randomly murder a somewhat despicable woman money-lender — to rid the world of her kind of vermin, simultaneously to rob her and do good with her money. His real motive? To prove that he can accomplish such an action, that he is above the laws that apply to the ordinary people around him, people trapped by the addictions of drink or gambling or poverty or just the "addiction" of muddled thinking. He commits the murder; it goes wrong. The money-lender's sister comes into the room when he is murdering the money-lender, and he must murder the sister too; in the event, he botches the robbery as well.

Thereafter, he is pursued by Petrovich, a senior police official who knows in his heart that Roskolnikov is the murderer. But, Petrovich never entraps him, instead allows him to dangle in freedom; Roskolnikov, whose guilt plunges him further and further into a kind of mental illness, at last confesses. He has come to know Sonya, a prostitute who has degraded herself to save her family. Roskolnikov is drawn to her (to her goodness, though he doesn't understand at the time that this is the reason for the attraction), and it is to Sonya that he first confesses; it is she who urges him to embrace her Christian faith and to confess to the world. He does confess to Petrovich, is sentenced to prison in Siberia, and Sonya follows him there; she takes up residence in the town where the prison is located. Roskolnikov's spiritual rebirth begins.

The plot is simple — though it is sometimes difficult for readers to focus on that simplicity, so rich is Dostoyevsky's portrait of the nether world, the dysfunctional world, of St. Petersburg. Yet within that incredibly rich panorama, his message is also simple: we all suffer. None of us is superior to anyone else; we achieve superiority only by serving others — as Sonya serves her family, as she cares for Roskolnikov's fellow prisoners; and only by loving others better than we love ourselves — as Sonya loves Roskolnikov.

Dostoyevsky's message to his own time and to the modern world in which he has had such influence: Be humble, there is moral regeneration possible through suffering; understand that God is infinitely merciful, merciful beyond our comprehension, that only Sonya — only the action of love — is what allows us to live our lives fully. When one considers the horrors that the alternative message has caused, it is obvious that Dostoyevsky's message is profound and eternal, one that still reverberates in the modern consciousness.

39
SIGMUND FREUD:
The Interpretation of Dreams

WHO WAS SIGMUND FREUD?

Austrian neurologist and psychiatrist Sigmund Freud (1856–1939), the founder of psychoanalysis, is best known for pioneering ideas that lead to a better understanding of human behavior. These breakthroughs in psychology led all of us to a more comprehensive view of human instincts, anxiety, repression, and defense mechanisms.

Born to Jewish parents in Moravia, Freud lived in Vienna for 80 years. He left after the Nazis occupied Austria in 1937 when he knew that his life, as a Jew, was in danger; he then sought safety in England.

He wrote: "A man like me cannot live without a hobbyhorse, a consuming passion — in Schiller's words, a tyrant. I have found my tyrant, and in his service I know no limits." His tyrant was psychology, and it took him into the dark corners of his patients' minds where he confronted the psychological entanglements of emotions and experiences that shaped their neurotic or psychotic personalities.

Freud studied at the University of Vienna. In 1886, he opened a private practice in Vienna where he began his experiments in psychology, using free association (Freud would say a word or phrase, then allow his patients talk about whatever occurred to them) in order to probe deeply into their minds. It was his belief that the mind contained hidden memories, which once uncovered would release the patient from any anxieties associated with these memories. His reasoning for using free association was that within the information he uncovered through free association some of the crucial memory contributing to the personality disorder would surface. In his probing into the human mind, he discovered that some information was blocked by resistance, which he wasn't always able to counteract. This realization forced him to search for other ways into the repressed regions of the mind. He turned to dreams, which he believed could be "the royal road to a knowledge of the unconscious activities of the mind."

In 1900 he published his book on *The Interpretation of Dreams.* According to

Freud, our minds preserve memories and emotions that aren't always known to us. Memories and emotions that exist for us during dreaming appear to us then in disguised form. By considering the fragments of dreams that we remember, it is possible for us to uncover repressed emotions. Freud believed that dreams were wish-fulfillments connected to sexual needs, and nightmares were anxiety attacks that these wish-fulfillments/needs might have caused.

Although his book received a cold response when it was published, Freud still believed that it was a significant breakthrough, and he once wrote, "Insight such as this falls to one's lot but once in a lifetime."

THE WORKS

The Interpretation of Dreams

In the late 20th century and early 21st century, the term "Freudian" has become one that almost involves derision. There are good reasons for this state of affairs. The profession of psychologist, which Sigmund Freud was instrumental in creating, now abounds in theories, and Freud's descendants do not necessarily subscribe to those of Freud. Psychiatry has made great strides in supplanting psychology as the scientific discipline devoted to the human mind, mainly because it is a branch of medicine, not of the social sciences. A psychiatrist is a medical doctor — and most psychiatrists now believe that mental disorders are in fact disorders of the brain and nervous system that can be most effectively treated by drugs — not the examination of the "unconscious" that Freud recommended. Even artists and intellectuals tend, these days, to see Freud's analysis of "mind" as more poetic than scientific.

In this context, it is difficult for modern man to comprehend just how influential Sigmund Freud really was in the years after World War I and for decades that followed. It is no exaggeration to say that Freud was regarded as a god, as a person who had almost single-handedly unlocked the mysteries of man's mental existence.

Many words and phrases in common usage come from Freud — Oedipus Complex, defense mechanism, the ego and id, repression, the unconscious, transference. How, anyone might ask, do they all "fit together" into a coherent theory or theories.

Freud's accomplishment was to offer an alternative to the Enlightenment dogma that man knows himself — Descartes's "I think, therefore I am" — the view that any man or woman knows who or she really is. Freud believed — and, as a doctor, he believed that his views were scientifically based — that the psychic dynamic in man is far more complex, that man represses certain wishes or desires (often sexual or violent in nature), represses them in the sense that they became part of man's unconsciousness, not the consciousness with which he lives each day. That mechanism sounds innocent enough — but Freud also believed that all neuroses (that is, all troubling behavior — troubling to both society and to the individual) was the result of this repression, its coming, so to speak, to the surface.

The solution was psychoanalysis — and, indeed, Freud has been called, and deserves to be called, the "Father of Psychoanalysis." Any patient — that is, a person suffering from a debilitating neurosis — can be helped by an objective therapist, who attempts, with the patient, to explore the unconscious. We are all familiar with the picture (it has been the subject of numerous cartoons) of a patient lying prone on a couch, talking about feelings to an objective therapist who sits on a nearby chair, tablet and pen in hand, taking notes, posing seemingly banal questions. Freud's view was that one of the ways that individuals recycle the dynamics of the unconscious was through dreams — and one of his most influential books is *The Interpretation of Dreams,* published in 1901.

Freud believed that the goal of his therapy — psychoanalysis — was to bring "to the surface" repressed thoughts and feelings, to help the patient develop, as a consequence, into a stronger, more self-aware person. The bringing of unconscious thoughts and feelings to consciousness is accomplished by encouraging the patient to talk, often via the method of free association. "If I say crocodile, what is the first thought that comes into your head?" — but also by talking about dreams that the patient can remember. It is this methodology that is most clearly explained in *The Interpretation of Dreams* — though, in fact, Freud constantly refined his theories in his subsequent books.

It is a curiosity that, though in many circles he is discredited, Freud goes on being immensely influential up to the present time. There is a perfectly reasonable explanation. Though many psychologists, and certainly most psychiatrists, no longer accept Freudian explanations of all mental phenomena, they accept more than they sometimes realize — as do we all: in a sense, we are all Freud's children.

In his writings and in his lectures, Freud introduced concepts that resonate; broadly speaking, they seem to us to touch on something we know instinctively to be true. Some of Freud's specific theories now seem to many people to be suspect: Do all boys at some point in their maturation have erotic feelings toward their mothers, at the same time that they wish to compete with, even destroy, their fathers (the Oedipus Complex)? And do all boys suppress such feelings? Most people would, now, shake their heads at such a proposition: If anything, it seems a little simple-minded, a little too pat as a means of accounting for a long list of human behavioral difficulties.

But, the central Freud precepts do strike any reader as valid — for example, that we are not completely aware of what we think and that we often act for reasons that have little to do with our conscious thoughts — our own actions often mystify us. Also, most of us know that talking out our thoughts to a neutral third party often clarifies our motives for us. From time to time, we have all had the thought that perhaps our motives and actions are more mysterious than we like to think — that we do not entirely understand ourselves.

It is this questioning that is Freud's greatest legacy — as is the consequence of questioning, that we can become more complete, better functioning men and women by understanding and mastering our unconscious thoughts and desires.

40
MAHATMA GANDHI:
The Story of My Experiments with Truth

WHO WAS MAHATMA GANDHI?

Mahatma Gandhi (born Mohandas Gandhi: 1869–1948) freed India of British rule by inciting his people to civil disobedience and non-violent resistance. His use of "satyagraha" — deliberate, non-violent resistance to tyranny through mass disobedience — has ever since inspired civil-rights movements around the world. In his autobiography, *The Story of My Experiments with Truth,* he clearly states his position on non-violence: "There are many causes I am prepared to die for, but no causes I am prepared to kill for."

Born in a rural area of India untouched by any foreign influences, Gandhi was taught by his mother the Hindu doctrine of "ahisma" (to do good, not harm). This belief, inculcated in him from early childhood, was responsible for his many non-violent acts against oppression. His technique for non-violent resistance (satyagraha) was used to fight against what Gandhi regarded as forms of tyranny — for example, the caste system, excessive taxation, foreign rule.

After receiving a law degree from University College, London, Gandhi returned to India and unsuccessfully attempted to set up a law practice in Bombay. In 1893, he was retained by an Indian firm with offices in Durban, South Africa. His experiences there shaped his future. Horrified by the South African government's blatant disregard of the civil and political rights of its Indian population, Gandhi actively campaigned against these outrages, all the while demanding basic rights for his people. He remained in South Africa for about 20 years; his activities there caused him to be imprisoned many times. The writings of the Russian novelist Leo Tolstoy, the teachings of Christ, and the essays of Henry David Thoreau (especially his *Civil Disobedience*) strongly influenced him. The result of his efforts was that in 1914 the South African government made important concessions to his demands; it recognized Indian marriages and eliminated an Indian poll tax.

Gandhi returned to India in 1916, and

after World War II he began his resistance movement against India's British rulers: his goal was home rule for India.

Although his fight against racism, colonialism, and violence established Gandhi's reputation internationally, the underlining reason for his actions has been often overlooked. A very religious man, Gandhi attributed his successes to the will of God. It was his desire to grow closer to God through the purity of his deeds — he lived simply, he lived to serve others. Gandhi, who had been subjected to so much pain in his life, found many answers in Hinduism: "Hinduism as I know it entirely satisfies my soul, fills my whole being."

Gandhi also said this: "What I want to achieve — what I have been striving and pining to achieve . . . is self-realization, to see God face to face, to attain 'Moksha' (Salvation). I live and move and have my being in pursuit of this goal."

THE WORKS

The Story of My Experiments with Truth

No one contemplating the early life of Gandhi would imagine that he would go on to become one of the most important political and spiritual leaders of the 20th century. Quite the contrary: he seemed destined for a life of obscure failure.

It is important, though, to understand the ways in which he did so. Such a description of Gandhi suggests that he was a firebrand, someone who was the driving force behind a bloody revolution. Yes, he was a revolutionary: such a description is true, but it is only half true.

Gandhi became the apostle, and the embodiment, of "satyagraha" — the resistance to and defeat of tyranny by one group of people over another through a kind of mass civil disobedience that completely avoids violence. His example proved decisive for those leaders of liberation movements who came after him — from Nelson Mandela to Martin Luther King Jr. — to the leaders of liberation movements — from those of women to those of sexual minorities to those of immigrants. All later civil rights and liberation movements took their example from him.

Gandhi defeated the British Raj, was instrumental in gaining independence for his country, using the method of refusing to cooperate with its oppressors. He tells his story in his autobiography, *The Story of My Experiments with Truth.* This title suggests that there was more to his philosophy and method than simple civil disobedience.

Gandhi believed that all wars, all destructive times in human history, were aberrations, that again and again the forces of human love and morality eventually win out. Though a life-long Hindu, he believed that all the major religions are forces for good that essentially believe in the same God. He believed, too, that no one who professed allegiance to God could do so and simultaneously ignore the moral demands of human life. That is, unless one practiced the "Golden Rule," there was no way that anyone could claim to be godly or religious.

In his autobiography, as in his life, he offers the radical proposition that the oppressed must live, must behave, in such a way that is more loving, more moral, than the lives of their oppressors.

Gandhi sets out, in *The Story of My Experiences with Truth,* what he regards as the components of a good and moral life. They are these: one must always devote oneself to the discovery of truth (as he said: "The truth is far more powerful than any weapon of mass destruction"); one must avoid violence to achieve worthy ends (though, he adds, if the choice is between cowardice and violence, then he prefers violence); one must live simply; one must strive for what is called "bramacharya" — spiritual and practical unity. That is, unity of the spiritual person with the person who must perform some kind of job, must raise a family, must be a member of society; and we must all embrace faith in God, knowing that at the core of all religions is the desire, the striving for, truth and love.

Gandhi was a great political leader, yes: he did what many people said could not be done. He freed his populous but weak country from the control of a small but very strong country by guiding the Indian people in ways that threatened to destroy the economy that the British had created. But the independence of India (and the subsequent partition of that India into Hindu India and Muslim Pakistan — a move that Gandhi vehemently opposed, and the conflict over which caused him to be assassinated by a Hindu zealot), happened a long time ago in the modern consciousness. His political triumph has now faded. What has not faded is his spiritual legacy — his vision of the "good life" as set out in his autobiography. It is one autobiography that all of us should read — for insight into the mind of one of the great religious leaders of modern times.

41
THOMAS MANN:
The Magic Mountain

WHO WAS THOMAS MANN?

Thomas Mann (1875–1955) is considered the most important German novelist of the 20th century. His writings deal with important political and intellectual concerns in Western society.

Born in Lübeck, Mann studied at the University of Munich, where he prepared for a career in writing. His epic novel *Buddenbrooks* (1901), which is a story about the decline of a family over a period of 4 generations, was largely responsible for his winning the Nobel Prize in Literature in 1929. In this novel, one of his great accomplishments is to dissect the lifestyle of the middle-class. Mann documents this lifestyle through various generations, showing very minor alterations — until the family yields to a modernity that is in conflict with its traditions and is ultimately destroyed.

Mann married Katia Pringsheim, a member of a prominent Jewish family, in 1905. In the early 1930s he began to denounce Nazism in an effort to create a strong resistance among the working class. When the Nazis took power in 1933, he and his family settled in Küsnacht, near Zürich, for safety, and in 1939 they left for America. In 1952, he left America when Senator Joseph McCarthy began his hunt for communist sympathizers, and he moved to Switzerland, where he later died.

During his lifetime Mann was the recipient of numerous awards.

THE WORKS

The Magic Mountain

From the humble beginnings of his life, few people could have predicted what Thomas Mann would become. He lived from 1875 to 1955; he was born in Lübeck to a German father, who was a grain merchant, and to a mother who had been born in Brazil. When his father died in 1891, his family moved to Munich where he attended university there, preparing for a career in journalism. Apart from a 2-year stint with an insurance company, he attempted to live by his pen — not in journalism but as a novelist and short story writer. In 1905, he married, he and his wife subsequently had six children (some of whom themselves became famous as adults), and his family continued to live in Munich until 1933. Then, his life became more adventuresome. Because his wife was Jewish, and because he disapproved of the Nazi regime, he moved to Switzerland in that year, then in 1939 the Mann family moved to the United States, where he taught at Princeton University. In 1942, the family moved to Pacific Palisades in California, and lived there until after World War II. In 1944, he became a citizen of the United States, and in 1952, he returned to Switzerland, where he lived until his death; he never lived in Germany again.

Despite this quiet life, which became more exciting only in its last 25 years, when he became a refugee, Thomas Mann was the greatest German novelist and short story writer of the 20th century. His works were widely translated, and were as well known and honored in the United States as in Europe; his fame was worldwide, and his accomplishment was acknowledged by the Nobel Prize in Literature, which was awarded to him in 1929. Yet, unless one has read his books, they seem, from the analysis they provoked, unusual "creatures" to have become world-classics. He is often cited for his highly symbolic and often ironic epic novels and novella-length short stories, notable for their insight into the consciousness of the artist and intellectual — artists and intellectuals who are usually European, most often German.

One has only to pose the question: Why isn't there a French or Polish or Italian writer of equal stature, of equal renown, to realize that Thomas Mann must in some way have been unique?

There are several reasons why this is so:

He was pre-eminently a great novelist, a great storyteller. In the sweep and drama of his novels, he is the rival of a Dickens or a Dostoyevsky — also their equal in his mastery of symbolism. He is, as well, master of a variety of prose forms.

The events of his life give resonance to his works. During World War I, he was a conservative; by the 1930s, he had become a liberal, an avowed enemy of the Nazi regime, and subsequently he became a leader of the refugee colony of German intellectuals in the United States. Moreover, he never forgave Germany, refused to live there again after the war — he became a symbol of those Germans who had not succumbed to Hitler. Because his experience — though on a more exalted, more intellectual, plane — mirrored the experience of millions of his fellow Germans, his works became fascinating even to those, especially to those, who had not experienced what being a liberal German, during the horrors of the 1930s and 1940s, had actually meant.

Finally, Mann tries to explain the first half of the 20th century to his readers; it is no exaggeration to say that he attempts to explain all of human history, before the 20th century, as well. No one has done it more brilliantly, from the exquisite novella *Death in Venice* to *Buddenbrooks,* the saga of a family over 3 generations (to an extent, based on his own family history), as brilliant and comprehensive as anything produced by the great novelist/chroniclers of the 19th century.

Though numerous of his short stories are still taught in world literature classes in American universities, it is probably his huge novel *The Magic Mountain* that is generally acknowledged to be his masterpiece; it is certainly his most famous work.

The Magic Mountain was originally written in 1912; it was then a brief novel or long short story — what is usually called a novella. His wife, suffering from a lung complaint, was treated at a sanitarium in Davos, Switzerland during that year, and the novella reflects Mann's impressions of visiting her there, where he got to know the team of doctors who were treating her. The coming of World War I interrupted his work on the book. He returned to it after the war, and, though he uses the same situation, he greatly revised and greatly expanded his book, converting it from a novella to a huge two-volume novel; it was eventually published in 1924. The sanitarium has now become the microcosm of the civilized world and the forces of perversity that caused the disaster of World War I.

His hero, Hans Castorp, goes to visit a friend who has tuberculosis, who is confined to a sanitarium in Davos, where he is hoping to be cured. Ironically, Castorp, during the visit, also develops symptoms of tuberculosis: his symptoms become worse, and in the end he himself spends 7 years in the sanitarium. World War I begins at the end of the novel; Castorp is conscripted; and, though this is not said overtly, the implication is that he will be killed on the battlefield.

During his "incarceration," Castorp endlessly talks with, and experiences, both the other patients and their doctors, all of whom are "spokespeople" of some aspect of pre-war and historic European notions, good or bad. The novel is what is usually referred to as a "bildungsroman." That is, a novel in which the hero is educated. In classical literature, a common element of plot has the hero visiting the underworld (the world of death) as a way of understanding (being educated to) the world of life. *In The Magic Mountain* the sanitarium serves the same function, as Mann says, commenting on his novel "One must go through the deep experience of sickness and death to arrive at a higher sanity and health." Simply put: one must experience the sanitarium — both our notions of good and our human notions and practices of evil — to learn how to live. Yet, in the end, Castorp probably dies. A cautionary tale? Probably a more accurate interpretation is that unless more of us are willing to examine our own beliefs, motives and actions, then we will, as a civilization, always end in conflict, war, and destruction. We pick up the pieces, start again, only to end up in the same place. It is too late for Castorp; it is not too late for the reader.

What can be said definitively about Mann was that he was a man of the world, a humanist, someone who believed that a man's life can be valued by how well he upholds the good in human civilization against the forces of barbarism: he believed, as he said, that life should be "led consciously, that is, conscientiously." We should all have read *The Magic Mountain* — to profit by Mann's vision of how man should live in order to create a better world, not a world that inevitably ends in horror.

42
ALBERT EINSTEIN:
Relativity: The Special and General Theory

WHO WAS ALBERT EINSTEIN?

The German theoretical physicist Albert Einstein (1879–1955) made important contributions to our understanding of physical reality. The greatest of his conceptions are his theories of relativity, which have become a model, a basis, for every physicist who has followed him. His speculations about energy and its relation to matter led the way to the creation of nuclear power and to the atomic bomb.

Einstein had an ordinary beginning. He was born in southern Germany to middle-class Jewish parents. At 15, he left his prep school and enrolled in the Federal Swiss Polytechnic in Zurich. In 1906 he received his Ph.D. from the University of Zurich. While at the Zurich Polytechnic, he met and fell in love with Mileva Maric, a Serbian physics student. This marriage, though of kindred souls, didn't last long; they divorced in 1919.

Also in that year, at the age of 40, Einstein became world famous, when the British Solar Eclipse Expedition confirmed his theory of general relativity: The gravity of the Sun deflected the stars' light rays exactly as he had predicted. Even today scientists marvel at his discovery.

In 1921, he won the Nobel Prize in Physics.

Einstein used his fame to champion what he believed were important causes — pacifism, Zionism, and liberalism. He once said: "It is important for the common good to foster individuality, for only the individual can produce the new ideas which the community needs for its continuous improvements and requirements."

THE WORKS

Relativity: The Special and General Theory

Albert Einstein is almost certainly the most famous person of the 20th century, and his fame endures into the current century. When the 20th century ended, *Time* magazine conducted a poll of its readers and staff to name the "Person of the Century." Einstein won. The runners-up were Franklin Roosevelt and Gandhi. Most people would agree that President Roosevelt rescued his own country from the worst Depression in its history, that he helped save the Free World from destruction by being its most prominent leader in the fight against Germany and Japan in World War II. Equally exalted claims could be made for Gandhi — that all freedom/liberation movements of the 20th/21st centuries begin and end with him, with his example, his actions and his pronouncements. Yet, Einstein beat out these two giants in the *Time* poll.

In a sense, there are two Einsteins — the scientist who 100 years ago published papers in a somewhat obscure scientific journal, scholarly papers having to do with what we now call "relativity" that irrevocably changed the way that man viewed the universe; and as well, there is the famous man, famous for being famous, who resided at Princeton from the coming of the Nazis until his death in 1955. He was bumbling, elf-like and charming in appearance, usually photographed wearing a moth-eaten sweater (having failed for months to have his hair cut), speaking with a thick German accent. He was, as more than one commentator pronounced, "cuddly." He might have been invented by Hollywood, and, more than any other public figure of his time, he was instantly recognized by the man in the street.

To most people, the latter Einstein is better known than the former Einstein — and most people also know the events of that Einstein's life — that he was the child of an obscure Jewish couple from southern Germany. He was educated at the Zurich Polytechnic, that, though he was a great womanizer in his youth, his romantic attachments were rather bizarre, that he devised his theories about "relativity" while working at a dead-end job at the Patent Office in Bern, Switzerland. Fame was suddenly thrust upon him when his theories were proven in 1919 (nearly 15 years after he published his famous papers). He left Germany when the Nazis came to power and came to reside at the Institute for Advanced Study at Princeton, a research institute/think tank specially created for him, which endures to the present time as one of the great scholarly research centers of the United States.

Because his theories had brought him fame, he was listened to, and it is important to remember in how many ways he was a force for good: Einstein was one of the great moralists of the 20th century, and, in retrospect, we see that he was right about virtually every issue on which he commented. During World War I, he signed an anti-war petition, incurring the great displeasure of the official Germany in which he worked. Later, in response to German anti-Semitism, he became a Zionist, yet at the same time he expressed his concerns about the rights of Arabs in any future Jewish state. Once resident in the United States, he urged America to military action against Hitler at a time when many Americans were isolationists. He helped many Jewish refugees come to the United States when such actions were not popular. He wrote to President Roosevelt, warning him that the Germans could conceivably, given German accomplishments in nuclear physics, create an atomic bomb, and, as a result, Roosevelt created the Manhattan Project, in which American scientists raced to produce the bomb before America's enemies could do so.

Although his theories were largely responsible for the creation of nuclear weapons, Einstein was horrified at what happened at Hiroshima and Nagasaki, and after the war he became a leader in the campaign for a comprehensive ban on nuclear weapons. He denounced Joe McCarthy, opposed the Cold War, and pleaded for an end to bigotry and racism. At that time, America was in a state of Cold War hysteria, and the response of many Americans was to regard him as innocent and naïve. And, to everyone's surprise, he maintained all of his life a belief in God, saying always that part of his life's work was to understand how the Lord had created and formed the universe that he, Einstein, had only described.

A formidable moral figure — yet there is also the other Einstein, the humble genius, the greatest scientific mind in a century in which the greatest scientific discoveries in the history of mankind were made. All the accomplishments of the era, for good or bad, bear his imprint — from nuclear power to the Big Bang to quantum physics to electronics — to, most important, the very structure of the universe. But all of us, 50 years after his death, tend to lose the great scientist by contemplating the great moralist, who was right about almost everything.

Yet his scientific genius was remarkable. It seems that, merely by thinking about it, about what troubled him, he came to conclude that the universe was not at all what it seemed — that it "operates" in a way very different from what anyone had thought before. His ideas are presented in full in *Relativity: The Special and General Theory.* Everything he thought or wrote thereafter was basically a footnote to these papers — as indeed is everything else done by the physicists who came after him. Most readers who do not have a scientific background in physics will find the theories presented in his scientific papers tough going — not so much because they are impossible to comprehend but because they ask us to comprehend our surroundings in ways that are foreign and strange to us. It is fair to say that, having read Einstein, almost anyone will require additional help from those hundreds of commentators who have attempted to explain relativity in layman's terms. The reader should not feel daunted in having to seek help. It took some of the greatest scientific minds of the last century years and years to understand Einstein's theories, to see the way in which they changed everything we knew, or thought we knew, about the physical laws of the universe.

Basically, Einstein proposes that distance and time are not absolute — as man has imagined from the beginning of time. Only light moves always at the same speed as an "absolute structure." Einstein proposed that gravity, as well as motion, can affect the intervals of time and of space. The gravitational force of a huge mass — for example, a planet — is so powerful that it has the effect of "warping" space and time around it.

Much of Einstein's later life was spent in trying to come up with a comprehensive theory — that which would unite all physical forces in the universe (even though his relativity principle is a fundamental criterion for all physical laws) — a grand "unified theory." He never succeeded, but his work paved the way for others — in ways they might never have imagined. All of us should try to understand him — by trying to read the famous papers, by choosing whatever commentary on those papers makes sense to us — because he can truly be said to have changed the world, and, however dimly, all of us should understand, or try to understand, why.

43
T.S. ELIOT:
The Waste Land

WHO WAS T. S. ELIOT?

T. S. Eliot (Thomas Stearns Eliot), who lived from 1888 to 1965, had in some ways a very conventional if privileged life. He was born to a rich St. Louis businessman and his teacher/poet wife, and was one of six children. His family's ancestors were from England, and the family had connections in the eastern United States as well. A distant cousin, Charles William Eliot, was President of Harvard University from 1869 to 1909. Eliot himself attended Harvard (he earned his B.A. and M.A. there, and would have earned a Ph.D. if he had shown up for the oral part of his examination), and he spent a year on scholarship at Merton College, Oxford. He was destined for a career as a philosopher at Harvard, having written poetry only as an avocation.

But his life was also unconventional. He decided not to go back for a second year at

Merton College, and instead settled in London in 1915. He never returned home to the United States but spent the rest of his life in England. He also married that year but the marriage was unhappy. Both Eliot and his wife suffered from nervous problems. He recovered but she spent the last 10 years of her life in a mental hospital, where she died. Eliot took a job in the foreign accounts department of Lloyds Bank in London, and worked there from 1917 until 1925, when he became a director at the publishers Faber and Faber, where he worked for the remainder of his career. In 1927, he became a British subject and converted to the Anglican religion (the official religion of the United Kingdom). The following year, in one of his books of essays, he describes his position as "classicist in literature, royalist in politics, and anglo-catholic in religion." His last major work of poetry, *Four Quartets,* was published in 1945, and thereafter, for 20 years, he published very little new poetry, though he did continue to write verse plays and essays. In 1957, he married Valerie Fletcher, 38 years his junior, who, after his death, became his executor, his editor, and the preserver of his legacy.

The Waste Land

T. S. Eliot had an unusual life, to be sure — but it was also an important one. Forty years after his death it is perhaps difficult for most of us to imagine just how important T. S. Eliot was during his lifetime — or how famous. He wrote critical essays that profoundly influenced a generation of readers and scholars. He wrote poems that still resonate, that most people would agree changed the course of modernist poetry. In 1948, he won the Nobel Prize for Literature; as well, he won most of the exalted literary prizes that England and America offer; and he was given the Order of Merit by the British Government — the highest honor that country confers. But this is most important: it is probably no exaggeration to say that he was the most influential poet in the English language in the 20th century.

What, precisely, was his accomplishment? Considering only the poetry (it is that which will endure); most people have found it complex, though, ironically, it is often written in very simple vernacular language and in free verse — it is non-rhyming, generally prose-like. The complication comes from the fact that Eliot, given his education and his life-long regimen of reading, was familiar with a vast number of writers, historical periods, languages and cultures. Thus, he may be quoting the Buddha; in the next line he is reproducing the conversation of a London barmaid. These different voices, and the huge range of different allusions, have confused people.

The reader may be reading five lines of language so straightforward that it seems like prose when, suddenly, there is a quotation from a medieval French poet.

It will be helpful for any reader to remember that Eliot is trying to create, in writing any poem, a synthesis of what has been thought and said throughout human history.

It is also helpful, for any reader coming to Eliot for the first time, to remember this chronology. For convenience, we can say that there are three phases to his poetry: 1) a period in which he expresses the disillusionment of the post World War I period — "the lost generation;" 2) Then there is the period, after his conversion to Anglicanism in 1927, in which he struggles with the intellectual difficulties of religious faith; and 3) Finally, there is a large gap in his writing of nearly 15 years (during which he writes *Old Possum's Book of Practical Cats,* which in turn, and much later, becomes the Broadway musical "Cats"). This period ends with "Four Quartets," the poetic cycle that most critics consider his masterwork, that which sums up all of his beliefs about life and religion, the relation of man to God.

The religious poems of the 2nd and 3rd periods are thrilling. It is impossible to read them without being moved, without examining one's own religious beliefs. But a modern reader might say: this is Eliot's solution to the problem of modern life, but I can be neither a classicist nor a royalist nor a convert to anglo-catholicism. For such a reader, the early works will almost certainly be more rewarding.

The Love Song of J. Alfred Prufrock, composed when Eliot was only 22, is the utterance of a middle-aged man who laments his inability to find anything meaningful in life, even as it is passing him by; he sees no spiritual or mental progress in his life; he is unable to connect, in love, with any other human being. It is one of the most dazzling debuts in our language. His next major poem, published in 1922, when Eliot was still a young man, is *The Waste Land.* It is one of the literary landmarks of the 20th century.

The Waste Land can best be described as Eliot's vision of the society he knew, a society he regarded as touching bottom — and, indeed, he said, after publishing the poem, that he was feeling his way to a new form, a new style, a new positiveness. Its central image is that of a fisherman (who is also royalty — an Everyman, in other words) fishing for meaning in life. And through a series of allusions to past cultures and to past writers and what they said in other periods of human longing, Eliot offers a definition of the disillusion felt by man in the 1920's. *The Waste Land* is deeply pessimistic, and un-Christian, and, in its lack of positiveness, deeply non-American. Many critics have called it the "first European poem" written by an American. In the poem, nothing provides solace — not sex, not love, not religion, not the past: God is nowhere to be found; the father of the world is dead; the fisher-king endlessly fishes without "catching" anything. As the last line of the poem says, Everything passeth our understanding.

If, as someone has said, the Modern Period begins with World War I — that is, a different world would have emerged after that war than what had been known before it — and if, too, that different world, that world in which we now all live, started in disillusion and personal heartbreak (there is no solace for the human consciousness in the poem), then *The Waste Land* may well be the most perfect — certainly the most explosive — expression of that beginning in disillusion of the modern period. Everyone should have read it — or should have tried to; and everyone should also remember that Eliot ended the quest that started in disillusion with one of the most positive religious poems in the English language.

Everyone will not of course end in the same place, but all of us know what it is to start any quest from a stance of disillusion, from a feeling of despair. *The Waste Land* is a great poetic statement of that bleakness that all of us, from time to time, have felt.

44
GEORGE GAMOW:
The Creation of the Universe

WHO WAS GEORGE GAMOW?

George Gamow (his last name is pronounced GAM-off) was born in Odessa, in what is now the Ukraine, in 1904. He trained at both the university in Odessa and subsequently at the University of Leningrad and became a prominent physicist and cosmologist in Russia, much respected by his Russian colleagues for his brilliance in the theoretical physics that he practiced. Although he was allowed to study at Gottingen and at the Theoretical Physics Institute of the University of Copenhagen (with time out to work at the Cavendish Laboratory at Cambridge University), Gamow became disillusioned with the oppressions of the Soviet Union, and he and his wife defected, in Brussels, in 1933, then moved to the United States in 1934. He worked at George Washington University in Washington, D.C., for 20 years, 1934–1954, spent a year at the University of California at Berkeley, 1955–1956, and ended his life's work at the University of Colorado at Boulder, from 1956 until his death in 1968.

THE WORKS
The Creation of the Universe

Throughout his life in America Gamow worked with a who's who of the West's most important theoretical physicists; he was responsible for bringing them together in annual symposia. He studied and contributed to our knowledge of such physical phenomena as the nucleus of the atom, the construct of stars, the creation of the elements, the genetic code of life, quantum theory and, most notably, the Big Bang Theory of the origin of the universe. In 1948 with Ralph Alpher, he published a paper, "The Origin of Chemical Elements" that described what came to be known as the Alpher-Bethe-Gamow Theory — a theory proposing, as proof of "Big Bang," the current levels of hydrogen and helium in the universe (thought to make up 99 percent of all matter). Those levels could be explained only as a result of reactions that would have taken place if the Big Bang had actually occurred.

In 1946, too, he postulated the existence

and the residual strength of background microwave radiation — again, a phenomenon that could be explained only by Big Bang (his speculation — that is, the existence of microwaves and their likely current strength — was later proved, in 1965). His contributions to this theory, and its refinements, are almost endless.

What is the Big Bang Theory? At its simplest, it holds that at one time, roughly 14 billion years ago, energy and matter were unbelievably condensed and that the "mixture" was almost immeasurably hot. This unimaginable concentration — call it the "original atom" then exploded (at that moment both space and time begin), threw out matter in all directions, which then coalesced into atoms. Which in time, created stars and planets and galaxies and eventually life itself, or just remained undifferentiated matter, all of which constantly retreats (the universe constantly expands) from the original "bang." Does this theory contradict religious belief — specifically, that God created heaven and earth, i.e., that God created the universe? Not necessarily. Most of the world's great religions have accommodated the theory. For example: Pope Pius XII was an enthusiastic early supporter of the theory, and the Roman Catholic Church has accepted Big Bang as a possible explanation of the origin of the universe. The reason for this accommodation is obvious: God's creating the universe in 6 days, then resting, is now widely interpreted to be a metaphor. Yet, whatever the origination of the universe, there must be a "first cause," that which made it happen, and the religious explanation is that the instigator (in this instance, the "cause" of Big Bang) is God.

Gamow's accomplishment in defining aspects of Big Bang, in other words, is a very substantial — but, with the possible exception of Einstein and his theories of relativity, most of the great advances in science in the 20th century have been collective accomplishments. A very large number of people has been involved in what we now know of the structure of the atom or the components of our universe and, preeminently, Big Bang itself. In some ways, almost all of contemporary theoretical physics is an attempt to refine the theory of Big Bang. Although he is sometimes cited as the "Father of Big Bang," that attribution is a mistake, one that only laymen, not other physicists, would make.

Gamow, amazingly, given that he seemed to work 24/7, was also the author of a number of books, and it is for these books that we most remember him today. His accomplishment in these books is substantial, because, in them, he did what many people thought could not be done. He explains in layman's terms some of the most difficult concepts in modern theoretical physics. So successful was he at doing so that Unesco awarded him its Kalinga Prize (for the popularization of science) in 1956. Two of his most famous books — *Mr. Tompkins in Wonderland* in 1940 and *Mr. Tompkins Explores the Atom* in 1945 — remain in print to the present day. Cambridge University Press brought out a combined edition of the two books, as *Mr. Tompkins in Paperback,* in the 1990s. In these books, Gamow creates an Everyman, an inquisitive bank clerk, Mr. Tompkins. He puts him through a series of adventures, the result of which is that the difficult principles of relativity and quantum theory are explained in a way that makes sense not just to adults but also to young people.

One, Two, Three . . . Infinity of 1947 attempts to explain modern science, from biology to crystallography, to the same audience. *Thirty Years That Shook Physics: The Story of Quantum Theory* is perhaps more theoretical but still comprehensible to the lay reader.

These are by no means his only books, and all of them will repay the modern lay reader, providing him or her with insight into the scientific marvels of our time. But it is perhaps *The Creation of the Universe* in 1952 (revised, 1961; reissued, 2004) that all of us should have read. For it is here that Gamow most cogently, most exhaustively, explains the Big Bang Theory (as well as the opposing, "steady state," theory of the universe). Obviously, a half century has passed since he wrote the book, and new discoveries are made about our universe on practically a yearly basis. Yet all of these discoveries are really confirmations of theories well known to Gamow (indeed, many of those theories were devised by him) at the time he wrote his book. For anyone wishing to know the basics of creation — and who does not? *The Creation of the Universe* remains our most comprehensible explanation and, for that reason, perhaps the greatest scientific text, for lay readers, about the modern scientific revolution in physics and about the way that we now view the universe.

45
SAMUEL BECKETT:
Waiting for Godot

WHO WAS SAMUEL BECKETT?

The Irish writer Samuel Beckett (1906–1989) wrote plays and stories about the human condition. Though they were sometimes laced with humor, most of his works are deeply pessimistic.

Beckett was born and raised in Dublin. He was athletic, excelled at cricket, and he went on to play successfully for Dublin University. At Trinity College Dublin, he studied Italian and French, as well as English, and later became a lecturer in English in Paris. While there, he was introduced to James Joyce who became both a good friend and an important influence on Beckett's work. In 1929 Beckett published his first work "Dante . . . Bruno. Vico . . . Joyce," an essay on Joyce's writing.

In 1936 Beckett settled permanently in Paris.

His two-act tragic comedy *Waiting for*

Godot, first presented in Paris in 1953, established him as a major international playwright, even though its meaning, and that of his other plays, have been endlessly debated.

Beckett received the Nobel Prize for Literature in 1969.

THE WORKS

Waiting for Godot

Many critics would claim that Samuel Beckett is the greatest playwright of the 20th century.

He was a true cosmopolitan. Though born and raised in Ireland, he went to live in Paris at the age of 30 and remained there for the rest of his life (he wrote in French, then himself translated his works into English). He was the friend/confidante of the great Irish writer James Joyce, who also spent a good part of his life in Paris and is himself regarded as the most innovative novelist of the 20th century. Beckett was far more diverse in his literary output than was Joyce. Besides a number of plays, Beckett also wrote well-regarded poetry and novels.

But it is his plays, in English, that have had the greatest influence on his times — and it is *Waiting for Godot* that is still regarded as the most important of those plays. It seems to have come from nowhere. He wrote two plays before Godot — one is lost; the other is known only to scholars, because it was never produced or published. Five years later, in 1952, he published *Waiting for Godot.* It was produced on stage in Paris the following year. He translated it into English in 1954, and it was produced in London and New York in 1955–1956. Since then, it has probably been produced at least once by every college drama department in the United States and Europe.

Suddenly, and ever since, the previously unknown Beckett became a household word. Why this acclaim? Because, more than anyone else, Beckett captured and defined an essential part of one aspect of the thought of the last century.

The play, in two acts, is very simple in its plot. In act one the tramps Vladimir and Estragon wait, by the side of a road, for Godot — they have an appointment with him. Pozzo and his sidekick Lucky turn up, and Pozzo taunts the two tramps, says that he owns the land on which they wait. They are followed by a boy who announces that Godot will not come today but will almost certainly come tomorrow. The second act is really a repeat of the first, except that, when they arrive, Pozzo has now gone blind, and

Lucky is mute. Although the play is interesting when read, and compelling when presented on stage — its language and images are stunning — it is essentially about things not happening. Finally, nothing really happens in the play, according to audience expectations of the "dramatic" — however cleverly it is presented, the play involves futility and inertia. At the conclusion the tramps decide to move on, but the play ends with their doing nothing, just staying where they are.

What does it all mean? The play has been endlessly interpreted, but most people agree that Beckett is dramatizing the tedium, repetition and pointlessness of human life. We deal with provocations, with events, but otherwise all we do is wait for some intervention that does not come — an intervention that will give our lives meaning (by Godot? by God?).

There is a recurring attitude among people of the Western world in the past century that is profoundly pessimistic. There are variants on this notion. Nevertheless, it seems to be the same notion, endlessly repeating itself. The notion has its beginnings, perhaps, with the disaffected intellectuals of late 19th century Russia — the "nihilists." World War I, with its disillusion-ments (it was a war, its participants came to feel, that had been fought for no purpose other than to enrich Western industrialists), which had in turn produced what the writer Gertrude Stein called the "lost generation," disaffected young people who railed against the world as they found it, lived only for gratification of the senses, believed that everything else in life was "meaningless." After World War II, the disillusionment was felt again — expressed by the "Beat Poets" of the day. And still the malaise continues — in the "live for money" attitudes of the 1980s, or in the rather more universal notions that "God is Dead" (never shows up, is always expected) and that the only way to live life is to regard it as only a chance for self-gratification.

Of course, there has always been, in all of this, a strain of utopian reform — thus the Russian Revolution, also an event of World War I, in which the attitude seems most to have been that if an economic system that benefited everyone could replace one that benefited just a few, then the world would be a better place. Or, a generation or two later, much of the world believed that if the empire created by that revolution could just be destroyed, then the world would be a better place — or if the industrial power structures of the West could be replaced by a system that exalts the individual, then we will all be happy. The century abounds in other such one-change-fits-all solutions. In our own time: If we can just defeat Muslim extremists, if we can just bring democracy to the Middle East, then the world will be a better place, and we will all live happily ever after.

But, despite these activist solutions, the passive solution is simply that life finally is meaningless, that one responds only to events (Pozzo and Lucky), that Godot is never going to arrive. This is the basis of the attitudes of the existentialist philosophers who became so popular after World War II — that, because human life is meaningless, because there are no determinants, because good and evil are simply human constructs, man must, to have any kind of purpose in life, invent himself and decide what gratifies him personally. Otherwise there is no hope — not from society, not from a Supreme Being: we will always be sitting on someone else's land, Godot will never keep his appointment with us.

But that somewhat positive approach to life of the existentialists (it assumes, after all, that if life has no cosmic purpose, it can have a personal purpose) is a step or two beyond what Beckett was doing. The great accomplishment of *Waiting for Godot* is that it defines the sense of helplessness, of purposelessness, that so many people in the last century have felt. Perhaps they go on to believe in new systems of government or morality. Perhaps they go on to develop new philosophical stances. The expression goes: If you've hit bottom, there is nowhere to go but up. Beckett, in *Waiting for Godot,* more tellingly than in any other modern work, describes what, for modern man, the "bottom" has actually meant. It is this facet of the work that most accounts for its enduring appeal — the beauty of its rendering of the "nothingness" that so many modern men and women have felt.

46
MARSHALL McLUHAN: *Understanding Media*

WHO WAS MARSHALL McLUHAN?

The place called "The Global Village" or the expression "The medium is the message" are now so much a part of our contemporary vocabulary that it seems as if they have always been there. But they didn't spring into existence on their own. They come to us from the life's work of Marshall McLuhan, a Canadian scholar and communications theorist who was a Professor of English at the University of Toronto from the end of World War II until 1979 (he died in 1980).

McLuhan was just as ordinary, in demeanor and career, as that description suggests. A native of Alberta, he did a B.A. and M.A. in English at the University of Manitoba, then did his work toward a Ph.D. at Cambridge University in England. There, he studied with I. A. Richards and F. R.

Leavis, two of the great gurus of the New Criticism, which holds that literary works are entities in themselves — stand-alone art works — that exist without reference to their writer's biographies, that are completely understandable as verbal constructs (edifices made of words). Their thought influenced him — but one can't push that influence too far. McLuhan is really unique. This mild and formerly obscure professor created some of the most influential scholarly works of the 20th century — notably *The Mechanical Bride* (1951), *The Gutenberg Galaxy* (1962), *The Medium Is the Message* (1967), and, perhaps most notably, *Understanding Media* (1964), works that utterly changed the way in which scholars, but also ordinary men and women, thought about the workings of the media, which have been so integral a part of all of our lives in the years since World War I. McLuhan, because of his writings, moved from obscurity to fame very rapidly. He was one of the world's most famous men in the 1960s and 1970s.

THE WORKS

Understanding Media

Ironically, given his popular fame, Marshall McLuhan is actually very complex. His writings have spawned an industry of commentators telling us what he was really talking about — which explanations are often themselves so complex that they require even further explanation. Yet, McLuhan's basic ideas — however he may have chosen to elaborate them — are actually simple and comprehensible to the ordinary reader.

McLuhan starts by saying that different kinds of media have characteristics of their own different from the content that they are actually delivering — hence the "medium is the message" expression. For example: The experience of reading *Gone with the Wind* is different from the experience of seeing the movie of the novel, which in turn would be different from seeing it as a play, as a theatrical presentation. If such a play existed — and all would be different yet again if various people were gathered in the same place, reading the novel on a gigantic television or computer screen. Yet the content is the same; it is the same novel, involving the same characters and scenes and incidents. From these differences in our experience of each medium, McLuhan concludes that different media must convey different messages (different from the content itself), which is another way of saying, as well, that our response must necessarily be different. As the human response is so different, could it not be said, Mc-Luhan asks, that each medium has characteristics of its own?

He further differentiates between "hot" media (that which requires very little participation on our part, just the participation of one sense) — for example, the movies. Or "cool" media, that which requires a great deal of participation, because not all facts are provided to us as in a picture book or comic book.

It is one of McLuhan's favorite tenets that our culture was originally, when it emerged from the barbarous to the civilized, aural and visual — the world in which writer/composers such as Homer would have sung or recited their stories to a group of listeners. They responded as if they were a tribe, a collective of people. This was a kind of revolution in culture. The coming of print creates another revolution. Suddenly man is coping with a medium on his own, not collectively, not tribally. This is one of the major revolutions in human experience because the advent of the solitary leads to the concept of specialization, to secularization, even to the notion of sovereign countries, which are a kind of specialization: we are German (i.e., have the consciousness of

341

Germans) as opposed to we are Chinese (i.e., have the consciousness of Chinese).

McLuhan believes that a third, and perhaps even more dramatic, revolution has taken place in the recent past and continues to the present time. The electronic revolution of the movies, radio, television, and the computer (though McLuhan precedes the world wide web, he anticipates it in all of his writings). Once again, and ironically, considering that most of us imagine these inventions to be great technological advances, McLuhan sees us as reverting to the tribe.

His description "The Global Village" has been much bandied about — to mean that the great miracle of modern media technology is that the world has been brought closer together. What McLuhan is saying is not precisely the opposite — but, he is much more pessimistic than most commentators about whether this kind of globalization is a good thing. He is warning that when electronic media replaces visual cultures (by which he means the culture of the printed word), then the tendency will be for mankind to move from individualism, from being "specialists," to a kind of collective identity. It is a very simple step, for him, from that prediction to this: That a world that has a collective identity — that is, one that is a "global village" — has the great potential to become a place where terrorism and totalitarian governments rule. If we are all the same, then we are easy to dominate — as if we were robots.

We need go no further than to contemplate television, in which packaged shows from advanced countries are shown round the world — never more comprehensively than now; or to contemplate the modern internet, which threatens to reduce all media (from books to recordings to movies to letters between individuals) to just one world-accessible single medium, to realize that McLuhan's concerns warrant our attention.

Finally he is saying this — and it is worth our contemplation: Any media technologies have an effect on our thought processes, which in turn affect how we organize ourselves socially. Print technology led to world wars between people who had organized themselves as nationalities or religions, but it also led to what is best in our culture: individualism and democracy. Are we quite sure that we like where the new technologies seem to be leading, which could well be the totalitarian state and, as he says, an atmosphere of constant violence? "Violence, whether spiritual or physical, is a quest for identity and the meaningful. The less identity, the more violence." His warnings are well worth heeding as we head further and further into the third great revolution in media.

47
ALAN TURING:
On Computable Numbers

WHO WAS ALAN TURING?

With regard to its stance on homosexuality, Great Britain is now one of the most liberal countries in the world. Homosexuals may serve in the military, they cannot be discriminated against in any commercial and social activities, and they are allowed to form and register domestic partnerships (the near equivalent of heterosexual marriage). Fifty years ago, in the years after the war, the situation was very different: homosexuality was a criminal offense. The scientist and mathematician Alan Turing (he was born in 1912), a homosexual, was arrested in 1952 in Manchester, where he was then a Deputy Director of the Computing Laboratory of the University of Manchester. His offense was that he had been sexually involved with another man. At one time, in 1943–1945, he had been head of Anglo-American efforts to break Axis codes, yet, as a result of his known homosexuality, he had already lost his security clearance. Turing was tried for this latest offense, convicted, and sentenced to forced therapy with estrogen, a misguided attempt on the part of law officials to "neutralize his libido." This barbaric therapy had a disastrous effect on him both emotionally and physically. In 1954, via the dramatic means of injecting an apple with cyanide, then eating the apple, he committed suicide.

His life became the basis of a successful biography by Andrew Hodges, *Alan Turing: The Enigma,* published in 1983. That book provided the inspiration for what became a well-known play by Hugh Whitemore called "Breaking the Code," which was produced in 1986. The title of both the biography and play refers to one of the great accomplishments of Turing's life — as the leader of a team in Britain's Department of Communications during World War II, he was directly responsible for solving ENIGMA, a German machine that produced codes that described Axis military operations, particularly their naval operations in the North Atlantic. "Breaking the code," most military historians agree, lead to the Allied victory in the naval part of the conflict.

On Computable Numbers

The tragedy of the end of Alan Turing's life (he died when he was only 42), and the posthumous fame that the famous biography and play accorded him (the play ran for 2 years, first in London, then in New York). The play drew on the more sensational aspects of Turing's life, have obscured the greatest accomplishment of that life — not that he broke the code but that he was, by any measure, the father of what is perhaps the most influential of all the inventions of modern life — the computer.

In *On Computable Numbers,* a book that he wrote when he was only 24 and just starting his work toward a Ph.D. at Princeton, he discusses, plants the seeds of, everything to which he would devote the remainder of his life — which is no less than the greatest single invention of the 20th century, the one that has most revolutionized modern life, has led to increased communications between businesses and individuals, and may be more responsible for the "globalization" of modern commerce than any other single factor.

Probably most modern readers — particularly those who are neither scientists nor mathematicians — will not be able to comprehend all of this book: it is enough to skim it, to "dip in" — to glimpse the breadth of Turing's thought — and to realize to what that thought led.

Here are some of the concepts that he later developed:

The Turing Machine is one that would read a series of ones and zeros from a tape. The ones and zeros described the steps that need to happen in order to solve a particular problem/task. A "program," we would now say. The Machine would read each of the steps and perform them in sequence — which brought the machine to the proper answer. This Machine, the concept of which he continued to develop after publication of *On Computable Numbers,* is essentially today's multi-task digital computer.

In fact, the breaking of the ENIGMA codes during World War II relied on a device, largely developed by Turing, based on his precepts, called COLOSSUS. The brilliance of ENIGMA was that, itself a kind of computer, it constantly changed the codes that the Germans were using. Just as soon as the Allies– had deciphered one German code, ENIGMA would change the code, and the Allies' work proved useless. COLOSSUS, a precursor of the digital computer, quickly deciphered whatever

ENIGMA could devise.

Turing continued his experiments with digital computers after the war — at the National Physical Laboratory — and developed the Automatic Computing Engine (ACE), one of the first attempts to create a true digital computer. In 1950 he developed what is now known as the Turing Test. It consists of asking both a person and a machine (a computer) a series of questions — at the point at which the answers do not differ, the machine may be said to be "intelligent" — and the Turing Test is now seen as the precursor of the concepts of artificial intelligence — as was Turing's article "Intelligent Machinery," which was published after his death, in 1969.

Turing continued his work on an Automatic Digital Machine when he moved to Manchester, where he worked on the Manchester Automatic Digital Machine (MADAM) and created an operating manual for his invention. Turing believed that by the year 2000 computers so sophisticated could be developed that they would in essence replace the human mind. That hasn't happened, but most computer scientists believe it is only a matter of time before such computers exist.

Turing was not only a very great scientist

— but also one of the great thinkers about the modern computer, if not the greatest one of all, the one who most deserves the title of its inventor. All of his work, from his mid-20's until his death at 42, has its foundation in what he writes in *On Computable Numbers*. It is one of the most important scientific documents of the 20th century — one that was destined to change the world in which we live and to cause Turing, now, to be regarded as the Founder of Computer Science.

48
SAUL BELLOW:
Henderson the Rain King

WHO WAS SAUL BELLOW?

Saul Bellow, who had a very long life (he lived from 1915 to 2005) is now widely regarded as one of the two greatest American novelists of the 20th century; the other one is William Faulkner. Bellow, of the two, had the more cosmopolitan life. A Jew, he was born in Canada in what is now a section of Montreal, soon after his parents had emigrated from Russia to Canada. To improve their position, to get better-paid work, his family moved to Chicago when he was 9 years old. Until he moved to Boston when he was nearly 80 years old — to take up a new academic position there — he was always associated with Chicago, and many of his most famous novels are set in that city. Despite his family's very humble start in the Chicago slums, Bellow was a reader who consumed everything he could put his hands on, and he was educated at both the

University of Chicago and Northwestern University. For years he was a member (professor) of the highly prestigious Committee of Social Thought at the University of Chicago, one of the greatest of honors bestowed by that university. He spent his life in reading and discussion, was the master of a variety of different subjects, was handsome and elegant in his appearance and demeanor, was an academic among academics at Chicago. In his personal life, he can be said to be one of the few Renaissance Men the 20th century produced.

Yet, if anything, he was even more of a Renaissance Man in his novels than he was in his person. He lived through most of the 20th century, and he tried to convey not so much its events as the psychology of his fellow human beings, whether his subjects were intellectuals, gangsters or frauds. His characters live in panoramic worlds that suggest the teeming milieu of Dickens. He was the master of a peculiarly 20th century "voice," one of his own devising, that ranged from the inflections of the Yiddish to the vernacular of the Chicago streets to the rhythms of jazz to the inflated speech of the most gifted of his colleagues at the University of Chicago. His accomplishment was recognized with the highest honors. He won the Nobel Prize in Literature, as well as, from his own country, the National Medal of the Arts and three National Book Awards. He was one of the few American writers who was as popular in other parts of the world, most notably in Europe, as he was in his own country, and there is some justice in the claim that, for the last half of the 20th century, Bellow was America's voice to the rest of the world.

THE WORKS

Henderson the Rain King

Because in his novels he held up a mirror to America, and expressed his vision in a peculiarly American idiom, Saul Bellow is well worth reading. It can fairly be said that any of his novels is worth our attention — for Bellow's unique vision of the world in which we live. His subjects are the isolation of modern man, his separation from anything that would sustain him spiritually, the possibilities, despite these difficulties, of a good and fulfilling life. These are compelling subjects to any modern man or woman who thinks rather than just survives.

Some critics would argue that *Henderson the Rain King* is neither Bellow's most profound nor most popular novel, but it outlines Bellow's characteristic themes in a vivid and understandable manner:

Published in 1959, *Henderson* explores both the post-war affluence and the postwar disillusionment of the 1950s in America, an affluence and disillusionment that continues to this day. Henderson is a millionaire — and a pig farmer. Thus, he is a representative of a simple man, yet at the same time his riches allow him to have any material possession he desires. In a sense, he is a kind of composite Everyman. But finally he has no desires — he feels lonely, despairing, estranged from the modern world, yet at the same time he searches for some purpose and meaning in his own life — and in modern life itself. Approaching middle age, Henderson feels only desperation, a sense of his own "deadness," a lack of connection with his life or with that of other people.

Henderson decides to make a pilgrimage to Africa, even though he has prejudices against African civilization (as "less advanced" than his own), to see whether a complete change of scene and cultures will cause him in any way to re-examine self and find new meaning in his life. After some misadventures, he arrives in a village that declares him Rain King. The villagers hope that he will soon make it rain, to counteract a drought. He becomes friendly with the king, Dahfu, and together they discuss various issues of life and death.

In these discussions, Henderson comes to a gradual transformation. He comes to believe that life is not so much an inevitable progress to death and decay; it is rather a series of constant rebirths — provided a man is willing to follow certain truths: That the relationship between the spirit and the flesh is a dynamic, not an antagonistic, one (put in different terms — body and soul are not enemies); that any rebirth, or self-transformation, must be accomplished by the human imagination; that rebirth spiritually involves a continual effort throughout our lives; and that love is the goal toward which all human striving should be directed. Our attitude should not be one of despair, a wishing to escape from human life; rather, it should acknowledge the wholeness of all being, and life should involve a constant spiritual growth — to the accomplishment of achieving love.

In the end of the novel, the rain comes, symbolizing rebirth. Yet Bellow leaves purposely vague what that rebirth may be, though Henderson plans, having returned home, to become a doctor — someone who will accomplish his own rebirth by helping others.

Although Bellow was to go on to write many more novels, to great acclaim, it is *Henderson the Rain King* that gives us the simplest expression of his philosophy of life — and serves as an inspiration to all those who, in modern life, have, like Henderson, reached what they regard as the end of the road. It is one of the more positive literary works of modern times.

49
NELSON MANDELA:
The Long Walk to Freedom

WHO IS NELSON MANDELA?

Looking back at the century just passed, many commentators have said that the 20th century was the bloodiest in human history. It is easy enough to imagine how such a judgment came to be. The first half of the 20th century involved two world wars; the second half involved conflicts between the capitalist West and the communist Soviet Union and China that, in their own way, were just as destructive of human life as the world wars had been. And compared to the tyrants of the past, the despots of the 20th century are now legendary for their mass murders: Hitler killed eight million Jews and millions more of the peoples of Eastern Europe; Stalin enslaved the peoples of Eastern Europe, killed millions of them, and killed millions of his own countrymen, those he imagined were enemies of the Soviet Union; Mao also killed millions of his own people. All three men had what they considered rational reasons for the killing — reasons that now seem to us barbarous, as if centuries of civilization had never happened. But they were only the Big Three. Other less renowned leaders, in positions of power — in Africa, Europe and Asia — engaged in mass murder on a lesser scale. If we think that the killing lessened as the century proceeded, we have only to remember that the horrors of Bosnia happened less than a decade ago.

It is easy, very easy, to be disillusioned about the 20th century — and to wonder whether the 21st century will involve more of the same thing, a fear that is hardly groundless. The century had barely begun when 9/11 occurred, and people in the West realized that they were engaged in a fight to the death with the radical forces of Islam.

Yet, in becoming disillusioned, it is easy to forget that there has been another, and very potent, current in 20th century life, which persists to the present — that of the fight for freedom. Whether that fight was embodied by the "underground" fighters in World War II or by the people of the United States who fought for the rights of minorities in the 1960s and 1970s, or by the brave people in the countries of Eastern Europe who, within living memory, rose up against their oppressors and toppled the Soviet Union, an act that only a few years earlier would have seemed impossible. The fight for human freedom in our time has been as important — and perhaps more significant in the long term — than have the battles that led to human destruction.

This human-freedom movement in the 20th century also produced its notable figures, whether it was Gandhi, inspiring his fellow Indians to fight the British Empire and, through passive resistance and non-violence, to gain freedom for his people as well as to provide a beacon for other colonial peoples. Or, in the United States, Martin Luther King Jr., inspired by Gandhi and by his own Christianity, to gain civil rights for all Americans. Of all of these life-affirming as opposed to life-destroying leaders, no one gained more fame internationally than Nelson Mandela of South Africa, who was born in that country in 1918.

THE WORKS

The Long Walk to Freedom
Whatever the insidiousness of racism, the hatred of one religion for another, or notions of class that have existed in many other countries of the world, these terrible

ideas were nowhere enshrined as overt government policy in the way that they were in South Africa — in the policy of "apartheid." Blacks, the majority of the country, were, by law and often violent practice, purposely kept in a subservient position to minority whites (the descendants of early English and Dutch settlers), who controlled the government, commerce and military forces of that country. Prevented from holding certain jobs, herded into ghettos away from the pleasant neighborhoods of whites, blacks in South Africa existed essentially as a slave class — in a world in which slavery had been officially abolished.

As a young man, Nelson Mandela, the son, then the ward, of tribal royals, tried the route of passive resistance, moral persuasion and non-violence chosen, too, by Gandhi and King, via the African National Congress, the group that eventually became the most potent force in the anti-apartheid movement. By sheer force of hard work, correspondence courses and attendance at a black university, he managed, with difficulty (he was essentially impoverished, on his own, disenfranchised from his family), to qualify as a lawyer and to try to help his people by providing them with legal advice (usually free). But eventually he came to feel that these actions were accomplishing nothing against the monolith of apartheid.

In the 1950s and 1960s Mandela became instrumental in reviving a stagnant African National Congress and its Youth League, and essentially turned the ANC into a terrorist organization, which fought the government of South Africa in a series of daring and increasingly violent conflicts.

In 1964, at the notorious Rivonia Trial, Mandela was sentenced to life imprisonment for his "crimes against the state;" he served for 27 years, most of it on Robben Island, where he began his autobiography, *The Long Walk to Freedom,* in 1974. His manuscript was eventually confiscated by prison authorities, but other prisoners had copies, and the manuscript survived. During those 27 years, Mandela became the most famous political prisoner in the world — an inspiration to his own people who refused to allow his legacy to die and a rallying figure for oppressed peoples and their sympathizers around the world who saw him not just as a symbol of anti-apartheid but also as a inspiration for all those people of the 20th century who were fighting oppression in their own societies. Mandela became an international hero, and "Free Mandela" was chanted around the world.

Finally, in 1990, through the intervention of the then president of South Africa, F. W. de Klerk, formerly one of Mandela's great enemies, Mendela was set free.

Together the two men, working together, devised the end of apartheid, and the coming of multi-racial democracy, based on majority rule, in South Africa; and together, they shared the Nobel Peace Prize of 1993. In 1994, Mandela became the first democratically elected president of South Africa, and he served until 1999; he retired in 2000.

After his release from prison in 1990, Mandela returned to his manuscript, completed his book, which was published in 1994 and became an international bestseller.

The Long Walk to Freedom is, of course, Mandela's own story, a memoir of his life, and it includes such poignant details as the necessary estrangement from his family in the service of his country. But it is more than a memoir. It details, as no other work has done, the path to freedom for South Africans. And not just South Africans. Mandela came to feel that the struggle of the blacks of South Africa was the story of all oppressed peoples, that the history of the destruction of oppression in South Africa was the story of the defeat of all oppressions, that his story, and South Africa's story, could inspire other fighters for freedom. In his Nobel acceptance speech, Mandela quotes Martin Luther King Jr., that humanity can no longer be tragically bound to the starless midnight of racism and war — and sees his struggle (and that of his countryman) as the struggle by all men for "genuine brotherhood and peace." His book has become a kind of monument to that goal.

50
YUKIO MISHIMA:
Confessions of a Mask

WHO WAS YUKIO MISHIMA

Japanese author Yukio Mishima (a pseudonym for Kimitake Hiraoka) was born in Tokyo in 1925 and died there — he committed suicide — in 1970.

Despite his short life, critics have compared him to some of the world's greatest writers — like Stendhal in his precise psychological analyses, like Dostoyevsky in his explorations of darkly destructive personalities (*Christian Science Monitor*).

Mishima spent his early years in the care of his grandmother, Natsu, who, though she lived in the same house as his parents, removed him from their care. A woman of aristocratic pretensions, Natsu was sometimes prone to violent outbursts, perhaps (according to some of the commentators on Mishima's life) the result of painful sciatica. Some also blame her for Mishima's fascination with death. While she cared for him,

Natsu also disallowed Mishima from engaging in traditional boyhood pursuits: he wasn't allowed to play sports or to fraternize with other boys. Instead, she kept him inside the house, alone or with his female cousins, playing with dolls. A frail boy, he was often ill.

At 12, Natsu returned Mishima to the care of his parents. They, too, provided a strange environment for a young man — his relationship with Shizue, his mother, bordered on the incestuous; his father was brutal, given to raiding Yukio's room and punishing him severely for creating what his father claimed were feminine manuscripts.

Alone, and fond of reading, Yukio devoured the works of such Western writers as Oscar Wilde and Rilke, at the same time that he mastered the classics of Japan. He published his first short story while he was still at school.

He was disqualified from military service during World War II, and spent those years in Tokyo. Because his father disapproved of his becoming a writer, Mishima wrote secretly while attending university and later while working at the Government Finance Ministry. His novel *Confessions of a Mask* made him famous overnight, and thereafter he devoted himself to his writings; eventually, he created an extraordinary volume of works in various genres.

After the war, too, he devoted himself to physical training and to para-military activities. On November 25, 1970, Mishima led a private militia of his founding in an attempted *coup d'etat:* they seized the office of the commander of Tokyo's headquarters of the Ground Self-Defense Force. The *coup* failed, and Mishima committed suicide.

His biographer and former friend, John Nathan, suggests that Mishima always suspected that his attempt at a *coup* would fail, that he was only using it to fulfill a dream of ritual suicide. Other commentators believe that it was his final and most dramatic attempt to protest against the weakness of modern Japan.

THE WORKS

Confessions of a Mask

The circumstances of the death of Yukio Mishima were so spectacular, so bizarre, that even now, more than 35 years later (he died in 1970), mention his name and you're very likely to be given a recitation of the facts of that death — rather than any mention of the accomplishments of his life.

Mishima, with a small group of four of his followers (they had formed a extremist group called Tatenokai — the Shield Society), took over the office of the commandant of the Tokyo headquarters of Japan's Ground Self-Defense Force, where Mishima had undergone basic training, held the commandant, General Mashita, hostage as a means of enforcing their demands, which were essentially that Mishima be allowed to address as many soldiers as could be gathered in the courtyard below the office. He made a speech to them from the commandant's balcony, a speech that could hardly be heard because of the noise of the crowd, the noise of surveillance helicopters overhead. It was intended to rouse them to a *coup* against the government, to restore the Emperor to his rightful place, in effect to re-make Japan into what it had been before World War II (though Mishima's Japan was, to an extent, a Japan of myth). Returning to the inside room after the speech, Mishima committed seppuku — ritual suicide — by plunging a knife into his own stomach, disemboweling himself, then Morita, one of his followers, as prearranged, attempted to decapitate Mishima; he botched the job. Toga, his second, finished off the decapitation of Mishima. Then Morita himself attempted seppuku — and Toga decapitated him too. This double suicide had other ramifications: Morita was widely rumored to be Mishima's lover.

Has there ever been so horrific, so incomprehensible a death, involving a famous writer? Probably not, and that death haunts the public imagination even now, so much so that we tend to forget what Mishima had accomplished, as a writer, in his short life of 45 years. He started writing as a child, and in his lifetime produced 40 novels, 20 collections of short stories, 20 books of essays and some 20 plays and screenplays. He was three times nominated for a Nobel Prize in Literature, was, obviously, considered a world-class writer, became more familiar to Western audiences than any other 20th century Japanese writer, and his last work, the 4-volume novel *Sea of Fertility,* an attempt to capture in fiction the history of 20th century Japan, is widely regarded as a masterpiece.

Yet, given the ritual suicide, the shock it gave the world, we have tended to concentrate on his life — that he was a frail and sickly child, that he was virtually kept prisoner in the family home by his grandmother, that he was a notorious homosexual, and that in his adult life he became obsessed with a strange cult of masculinity of which ritual suicide was a part. Some of this myth is true; most of it is just sufficiently untrue as to be misleading. For example: People who knew him best say that his homosexual liaisons were few and far between; also, he married in 1958, remained married to that woman until his death, and had two children to whom he was devoted.

Confessions of a Mask is a youthful novel (he was only 24 when it was published), and, because it reads as if it must be autobiography, it has become, given the strangeness of his life and death, Mishima's most popular work. It is a novel about a young man growing up in wartime: Mishima was 16 at the time of Pearl Harbor; he could have served in the closing years of World War II, got himself a deferment by lying, spent the war years in bomb-ravaged Tokyo. In the first half of the book, he describes the progress toward his acknowledging that his erotic interest is in men; the second half describes his relationship with a woman, Sonoko, for whom he feels a platonic, rather than a sexual, love. From the evidence of this book, readers have concluded that Mishima is confessing to a homosexuality that, given the dictates of Asian society at the time (they persist to the present day), must be hidden behind a "mask." Everything else he contemplates in the book is reduced, by many readers, to just this admission of sexual deviancy.

But that is a very superficial reading of *Confessions of a Mask*. The frail sensitive young man — the man who would become a famous writer — is always playing with, considering, a kind of machismo that at the time seems anachronistic. He idolizes the male body, but in a particular way; it is an idealized body (and, indeed, Mishima thereafter became an obsessive body-builder, transformed himself into his own vision) — the body of a warrior, a throwback to the old samurai class of Japan. Into this mix, there is an aspect of homosexuality that is itself historic — the semi-mythical notion (it persists from Ancient Greece) of warriors who are themselves lovers. As well — drawing on other legends — such warriors are often called upon to make the supreme sacrifice to make a dramatic point, to set an example for the public good.

If these particular notions sound familiar to readers, they should remember that they savor of fascism, of some of the precepts of Nazi Germany — then readers should remember too, though often this is less familiar to us, that Japan was also, in World War II, a fascist, militaristic state, allied with Nazi Germany against the Allies.

THE IMPORTANCE OF MISHIMA

And the lessons for us today? The concept of the superman, from its beginnings in the works of the philosopher Nietzsche, goes on to pervade the thought of the Western world in the 20th century. This concept undergoes sea changes; in the end, it is a corruption of what Nietzsche was actually saying. But the received version goes like this: that there are people who are superior to others, or ethnic groups that are superior to other ethnic groups (think the German view of Jews or any Slavic peoples). As well, it is a superior military class (the S.S.) that will enforce the will of the superior race — who will, if necessary, die for the glory of the Fatherland, to prove both their own nobility and that of their cause.

One of the lessons to be learned in reading *Confessions of a Mask* is that these concepts were not peculiar to the West, that a Japanese man could feel the same way, that such concepts occurred in Japanese society as well in those societies with which we are more familiar. But there is a further lesson here: Mishima wrote most of his works, embarked on his crusade to become a modern samurai, *after* World War II had ended. Japan, with its emperor, with its warrior class, with its industrious, religious and highly educated people (as gifted in their own way as the Germanic classes of central Europe), had in fact lost the war — to the superior technology and know-how of the Allies, people regarded by the cultivated Japanese as cultural inferiors. The great cities of Japan, hence its culture, lay in ruins, and in Mishima we find all the resentments of a subjugated people. The difference was that he was a writer of genius; he had a voice. More: The response of subjugated peoples is often simply to accept subjugation. In his case, Mishima dreams of renewed glory — of making Japan strong again by reverting to the past, the past of a God-like Emperor, and of a warrior class of beautiful and selfless men who will insure that greatness.

It could be said that many, if not most, 20th century intellectuals succumb to nihilism, the view that nothing matters, nothing is of consequence. There is, though, a different current in our times — to spread democracy, to relieve the agonies of the poor and sick, or, in Mishima's vision, to restore a lost (and to an extent mythical) world that was greater than the world in which we live. Mishima, however misguided he may have been, is not the first and he certainly will not be last to have such dreams — and his *Confessions of a Mask* is the perfect expression of a longing for greatness, for nobility, that, even as we enter the 21st century, refuses to die.

APPENDIX

As readers are urged to sample the great literature of the world, the following list is simply a sample of versions of each book as found online. Prices and availability may change. Naturally, there are multiple versions of almost every title; in addition, readers will find critical commentary and abridgments of larger works.

The Bible There are many versions and translations of *The Bible,* with a variety of emphases. For simplicity, we have included two standard versions:

The New Jerusalem Bible: Standard Edition (Doubleday, 1999), 1,424 pages, hardcover. Traditionally considered a Catholic edition.

The Holy Bible King James Version: 1611 Version (Hendrickson Publishers, 2003), hardcover. Traditionally considered a Protestant edition.

The Odyssey of Homer (Harper Perennial Modern Classics, 1999), 384 pages, paperback.

Confusiansism — The Analects of Confusius, Volume 4 (Harper Collins, 1992), paperback.

The Oresteia (Oxford University Press, USA, 2004), 304 pages, paperback.

The Histories (Oxford University Press, USA, 1998), 840 pages, paperback.

The Republic (Penguin Classics, 2003), 496 pages, paperback.

Aristotle's Metaphysics (Green Lion Press, 1999), 369 pages, paperback.

Mahabharata: The Greatest Spiritual Epic of All Time (Torchlight Publishing, 1999), 944 pages, hardcover.

Euclid's Elements (Green Lion Press, 2002) abridged edition (original work is 13 volumes), 529 pages, paperback.

On the Good Life (Penguin Classics, 1971), 384 pages, paperback.

Lucretius: On the Nature of Things (Focus Publishing, 2003), 256 pages, paperback.

The Confessions of St. Augustine (Revell, 1997), 208 pages, paperback.

The Koran (Penguin Classics, 2004), 464 pages, paperback.

The Arabian Nights: Tales from a Thousand and One Nights (Modern Library, 2001),

912 pages, paperback.

The Tale of Genji (Vintage, 1990), 384 pages, paperback.

The Song of Roland (Kessinger Publishing, 2004), 144 pages, paperback.

Aquinas's Shorter Summa: Saint Thomas's Own Concise Version of His Summa Theologica (Sophia Institute Press, 2001), 432 pages, paperback.

The Adventures of Marco Polo (John Day Co., 1948), 193 pages.

The Divine Comedy: Inferno, Purgatorio, Paradiso (Everyman's Library, 1995), 960 pages, hardcover.

Canzoniere (Routledge, 2002), 335 pages, paperback.

The Canterbury Tales (Penguin Classics, 2003), 528 pages, paperback.

Le Morte d'Arthur: Complete, Unabridged, Illustrated Edition (Cassell Illustrated, 2003), 1088 pages, paperback.

The Notebooks of Leonardo da Vinci (Oxford University Press, USA, 1999), 432 pages, paperback.

Utopia (Penguin Classics, 2003), 176 pages, paperback.

Martin Luther's 95 Theses (Arch Books, 2004), 128 pages, hardcover.

Montaigne: Essays (Penguin, 1993), 416 pages, paperback.

Don Quixote (Ecco, 2003), 976 pages, hard-cover.

Hamlet (Washington Square Press, 2003), 400 pages, paperback.

The Dialogue Concerning the Two Chief World Systems (Modern Library, 2001), 640 pages, paperback.

Two Treatises of Government and a Letter Concerning Toleration (Digireads.com, 2005), 180 pages, paperback.

The Principia (Prometheus Books, 1995), 465 pages, paperback.

The Wealth of Nations (Modern Library, 1994), 1,200 pages, hardcover.

Jefferson: Political Writings (Cambridge University Press, 1999), 684 pages, paperback.

Selected Poems of William Wordsworth (Grey Walls Press, 1947), paperback.

On the Origin of Species: A Facsimile of the First Edition (Harvard University Press, 2005), 540 pages, paperback.

Great Expectations (Oxford University Press, USA, 1998), 544 pages, paperback.

The Communist Manifesto (Signet Classics, 1998), 96 pages, paperback.

Crime and Punishment (Bantam Classics, 1996), 576 pages, paperback.

The Interpretation of Dreams (Kessinger Publishing, 2004), paperback.

Gandhi an Autobiography: The Story of My Experiments with Truth (Beacon Press, 1993), paperback.

The Magic Mountain (Vintage, 1996), paperback.

Relativity: The Special and General Theory (Penguin Classics, 2006), paperback.

The Waste Land and Other Poems (Harvest Books, 1955), 96 pages, paperback.

The Creation of the Universe (Dover Publications, 2004), 160 pages, paperback.

Waiting for Godot (Faber and Faber, 2006), 96 pages, paperback.

Understanding Media: The Extensions of Man (The MIT Press, 1994), 392 pages, paperback.

The Essential Turing: Seminal Writings in Logic, Philosophy, Artificial Intelligence, and Artificial Life Plus the Secrets of Enigma (Oxford University Press, 2004), 622 pages, paperback.

Henderson the Rain King (Penguin Classics, 1996), 352 pages, paperback.

Long Walk to Freedom (Abacus, 2003), 480 pages, paperback.

Confessions of a Mask (New Directions Publishing Corporation, 1958), paperback.

ABOUT THE AUTHOR

George Walsh, formerly of Fitzroy Dearborn Publishers, is an award-winning editor and writer, having won numerous awards from the American Library Association, among others, for his research and reference books. He has written and published with Socrates Media, Reference Services and St. James Press.